*A Miraculous Breathtaking **True Story**
of **My Supernatural Encounter with God!***

OVER THE SEA
AND
OVER
THE SUN

*Very Unique Miracles, Signs, and Wonders from Heaven...
This is something only God can Do!*

CAROL WARDEN

outskirtspress
DENVER, COLORADO

The Devotional Bible 2003 Thomas Nelson, Inc.

"Scriptures quoted from The Holy Bible, New Century Version, copyright, 1987, 1988, 1991, by Word Publishing, a division of Thomas Nelson, Inc. Used by permission."

The Publisher is pleased hereby to grant permission for the New Century Version to be quoted or reprinted without written permission with the following qualifications: (1) up to and including one thousand (1,000) verses may be quoted, except: (a) the verses being quoted may not comprise as much as 50 percent of the work in which they are quoted, and/or (b) the verses quoted may not comprise an entire book of the Bible when quoted.

The Devotional Bible was produced with the assistance of Karen Hill, Administrative Editor to Max Lucado, and The Livingstone Corporation (www.LiningstoneCorp.com).

Outskirts Press, Inc.
http://www.outskirtspress.com

ISBN: 978-1-4787-5709-2

Outskirts Press and the "OP" logo are trademarks belonging to Outskirts Press, Inc.

PRINTED IN THE UNITED STATES OF AMERICA

In Loving memory of my brother:

Richard Keith Warden

August 7, 1957 – June 6, 2012

CONTENTS

1

PROLOGUE

After the loss of my mother at the age of six, I became very skeptical about whether God was real. I lived my entire life unsure, until one night on May 18, 2011, when I asked Jesus to come into my life by saying the Salvation Prayer; and that is when everything changed! I began to experience the Supernatural Power of God Almighty for the first time in my life right here in my home.

This is a phenomenal and very personal, emotionally breathtaking True Story; that by no means is a tell-all about my life. The focus point is all about the "Supernatural Power of God" that has been revealed to me through the Holy Spirit, the Gifts of the Spirit, and Prophecy that manifested during a crisis in my brother's life and mine. Together, God gave us victory over death, and I feel compelled to share these very unique miracles, signs and wonders that are from heaven with others, so they may know the true love of God, the Lord Jesus Christ and the precious life changing fellowship of the Holy Spirit, with the evidence of speaking in tongues (other languages).

Supernatural events that I did not know were even possible or unheard of happened; the gifts and profound miracles that took place have forever changed my life and those around me. In this book, is the first time I have ever shared any of these photographs with the public, unless it was a close friend or family member and when I was sharing my testimony with someone to lead them to the Lord; **because it is Holy!**

Throughout this story, after I ask Jesus to come into my life, you will see for yourself how God begins to pour out His exponential blessings into my life. I know that you will find this story to be heart felt and inspirational, because these profound miracles that I received are all specific prayers that I asked of God that He honored! What I am about to share with you, can and will change your life too!

I have appropriately provided Biblical Scripture throughout my story, including the Gospel Soul Winning Scripture, to educate those of you who don't yet know the Word of God, and to encourage those of you who do. While I am still learning every day, I want to enhance your life, by sharing with you the things I have learned about God's Word; how His Word is true and how He does what He promised!

2

~~

LOSS AND HOPE

As very young children, my brother and I lost our mother in a car accident on New Year's Eve; she was only twenty five years of age, and my father was twenty six. I was six years old and my brother was seven. My father had borrowed his cousins Convertible GTO to celebrate this particular New Year's Eve. They had slid on Black Ice, and the passenger side of the car hit one of those large green metal telephone poles; causing a fatal injury to my mother's head. She was alive for twenty four hours in the hospital, while my father was in a Coma in another room. I remember being told, my mother would look at the pictures of my brother and I and pray to God that one of them would live. Our father was in a Coma for about a week, which at the time seemed to me like two months as I remember; he had survived and later he finally came home, thanks be to God we still had our father. This as you can imagine changed our lives forever. Needless to say, life as we knew it would never be the same again.

When my brother and I were told of her passing and how it happened, we were both in disbelief and I said something horrible that I will never forget and have since repented for it as an adult. I was so distraught that I remember saying "I hate God!" I was only six years old, and I was hurt, scared, mad and confused. From that moment on I must admit, I became very skeptical about all of the good things I had heard about God, and because it was so painful, no one ever spoke about the tragedy ever again. My father eventually remarried and we had a big happy family of four girls and two boys. This became the healing part of our lives together as a family again. We even moved to California for a fresh start; I can remember my brother and I taking the church bus and he and I would go to Tent Revivals with our friends who lived in the neighborhood.

Our grandmother Belva Whitehead from Lebanon, Tennessee; was a Spirit filled and faithful woman of God, she is who I remember as being one of the most influential people in my life with regards to the Holy Bible and the power of God. I went to church with her when I was a little girl and saw many people touched by the power of God. At that age I only knew God through her, but I knew enough to know that nothing was impossible with God and she would tell me of the visions that God would give her...and I believed.

As many seasons and years past we eventually moved back home to Lebanon, Tennessee; where my father Ron Warden and my uncle Luther Hudson opened R & L Body Shop together. As a young teenager I stopped going to church, after all no one else in my family was going either. Sadly throughout my life I still found myself unsure of the things of God and if he was real, because of so many more deaths, divorces and other tragedies I won't mention here, that we all have had to endure in life not only in mine, but my whole family and of relatives families and friends around us. But don't get me wrong, there were many wonderful years and blessings that we did have; with such a big family there was never a dull moment, lots of love and Christmas time was always very big and exciting in our house. My father Ron and my uncle Luther eventually changed the name of the Body Shop to "American Auto Body" in Lebanon, Tennessee; and it is still there and in the family today. Looking back now, I don't know how my dad did it all, providing everything we needed for a family of eight. And we all have some very special, happy and fond memories of our childhood that we still cherish and reminisce about to this very day.

Just out of high school, my brother Rick joined the Navy and served our country for ten years, going on to fulfill his passion for cooking as a graduate from Johnson and Whales Culinary School, he was a Pastry Chef following his dream. I left Tennessee going out on my own as an independent woman in my early twenties yearning for adventure and just wanting a new direction to change my life, while the rest of the family remained in our small country town. During this time cell phones did not yet exist or computers, so there was no texting and sending photos, to keep in touch we wrote letters and occasionally called our loved ones, our phone calls were like a visit catching up on things we had done and encouraging each other with love, while our hearts yearned to be near our family, and trying to be somewhat accomplished often times can take you away. I have always called Tennessee home; and I have almost always returned for the holidays if I could. Coming home to see and be near my loved ones has always been so special to me, missing my family terribly over a period of twenty six years now. I call it a "Tennessee Christmas" nothing like it; family and friends sitting around the fireplace singing and playing their guitars is so wonderful, I could stay up all night long listening and visiting enjoying every minute. I returned home to live off and on a few times over the years and left again. My father and step mother divorced when I was a freshman in High School and this had brought much despair to my younger siblings, it had broken our family completely apart and was very troubling for us all, each of us going our separate ways as very young adults and some starting families of their own.

Then my father was shot and murdered at the age of fifty one; we were in shock and devastated, our dad our rock, our world was gone and our lives fell apart. My brother Rick started to undergo treatment for Manic Depression and PTSD, better known as Post Traumatic Stress Disorder, at that time this was something rarely heard of, at least to my family anyway. None of us really understood it at first, but over the years we began to see the struggles my brother was dealing with and we learned through him over time what was really happening. And since the loss of our father, I believe it was just too much for him to bear and he was deeply affected in a way that was hard to understand. I saw how it had burdened my brother's life and my heart was broken for him. But again, picking up the pieces of our lives we had to carry on; even though we were apart, my siblings and I have always remained close with tremendous love for one another. Looking back, I can see how the loss of our father has deeply affected every one of our lives.

Finally, I found my calling and got into Residential Property Management starting in the Antioch, Tennessee area in the eighties, when new construction properties where going up right and left all along Bell Road; and this became my career for twenty years; traveling and living in New Orleans and Lafayette, Louisiana, St. Louis, Missouri, South Florida, New York City and on to Plymouth, Massachusetts. At the age of forty I pursued a Real Estate Sales Director opportunity for an entire year and finally became "Sales Director" for a Custom Home Designer and Builder. My "dream job", working at a three thousand acre Master Plan Community located in Plymouth, Massachusetts, where I was extremely successful for five years competing with eleven other builders, selling half acre land parcels for up to $250,000.00, and designing and building custom homes in the price point of $650,000.00 to just over a million, it was a great ride, but deep down inside I felt something was still missing; I was earning more money than I had ever earned in my lifetime and I worked very hard for it and it was rewarding but yet I still felt empty inside, not completely fulfilled.

The economy started to turn in 2006 and my "dream job" ended; so I revaluated my life and decided to move back to South Florida, where I had previous lived for ten years, and where the sun always shines. I knew there would be plenty of opportunities with new construction booming and with my accomplished resume, I wouldn't have any trouble getting a job, but I was wrong. A year later I was still looking, it was as if everything had frozen in time. Construction stopped and nothing was happening except for cut backs and layoffs. But as always I kept a good attitude and pursued...meanwhile money was going out and none was coming in and I was getting scared, looking for a job became a full time job.

One morning on June 18, 2007, I awoke to go about my usual day seeking a career opportunity and I noticed my Toy Pomeranian Nigel's eyes were half closed, when he looked up at me it was as if his little eyes were just burning. After a few hours I could see his condition was not improving. I called my veterinarian and they told me to bring him in; I got into the car holding him, he is only 7 ½ pounds so I usually held him or he sat on a pillow in the passenger side; on the way to the veterinarian I was hit by an 82 year old woman who was coming across the medium while I was going 45 miles per hour. I was hit in the driver's side rear which accelerated me off the road, head on into a large solid square concrete pole on the street corner. The impact was so intense that my elbow went through the driver side window and ejected Nigel my Pomeranian out to the street! It happened so fast I didn't see it, when we crashed into the concrete structure I was in shock and did not know it; I looked to my side for Nigel and he was gone, then I heard him make a squeal and looked and their he was standing on all fours out on the street. I was in a panic, kicking my jammed car door open so I could get to him before he got run over, adrenalin pumping, I could not believe we were both alive, my car which happened to be an older Mercedes was totaled and the fire department rescue unit said that car saved my life. I was crying hysterically, holding Nigel because I was afraid he might be bleeding internally, some blood coming from his mouth and my left arm with lacerations, blood was dripping on me and the ground. A very nice lady got out of her car and offered to take him on to the veterinarian for me; after getting her phone number and address, driver's license etc., I allowed her to do so. That's where I was going in the first place and it was nearby.

This dear lady that hit me was later diagnosed with early Alzheimer's and was lost. Her injuries were a broken wrist and mine were Cervical Spine Injuries and Thoracic Spine Injuries resulting with a total of five herniated discs in my neck. Because I was unemployed at the time, I did not have health insurance and I was in need of medical attention. I retained an attorney and thus the long and painful journey began.

Thankful that my baby Nigel survived without a broken bone and that I was not paralyzed or worse,

I began with seeing doctors for an explanation of my injuries and pain management, MRI's and so on. Meanwhile, I was paying cash for all of my prescription medications on top of all my other bills while having no income coming in. Not really understanding the level of injuries I had at this time, I knew I must keep pressing forward for a job or I was going to be broke very soon.

During this process I developed chronic pain, depression and anxiety. I was taking medication for all these things and finally got hired as an Activities Director for a Fifty Five Plus Community here in South Florida; sadly I started to realize I just could not do the normal things I could do before and there was so much politics going on. Six months later I found another opportunity in Residential Property Management which I had done previously for twenty years; this job just about literally physically killed me because of my injuries, but I tried my best not to show it; while they were looking for reasons to fire me and could not find any, my supervisor began to harass me to a point that I had to address it with her and ask her to back off so I could do my job. It was the most unprofessional experience I have ever endured in my entire career. It turned out the reason for the harassment being, so the president of the management company could hire his best friend, who had no experience, whom I trained during that time only to come in and take my position twelve months later, I was stressed to the max!

Because of the economy so many people were starting to hire friends and family so they could survive, we were in a depression and no one in our generation had ever experienced anything like this recession before.

After that, going on five years of monthly doctor's visits and daily medications, having to make them stronger and again no health insurance, I had to pay cash out of my pocket; I was in a bad situation. Finally, I did win my settlement after two years; by this time not counting what I had to pay to my attorney, prescription medications and medical bills there wasn't much left and I still had injuries to deal with. I also had to move again because part of my compensation with the property I managed was living on site and included as part of my benefits.

So as you can imagine by this time, I really needed a break to say the least. I have always been a very optimistic person throughout my life, even with my hardships, having a positive mental attitude was how I survived.

I got settled in to a new place, happy to start over and with my chronic pain and stress, depression that I could not beat set in...I was in a very dark place and nothing was working. In fact, it was a little scary because I could not control it in my mind and that is not a place that I had ever been before.

I was still seeing my Orthopedic Surgeon on a monthly basis and this time, I had a full on melt down, my Dr. put me on anti-depressants because he said that the chronic pain I was having was also causing my depression. Six years later after my car accident I am suffering more than ever, while one Dr. recommends no surgery due to that fact that it may make my injuries worse, and another Dr. recommends three different levels of surgery on my neck and now my lower back! I'm miserable, but stable and my pain is being managed. I said no!

Although I have always been very independent, I started to feel very alone and sad, I really needed to turn to someone for help, but I had no one around to talk to about what I was going through, and all of my family living in Tennessee, I had no help with anything; I hadn't made myself available for dating in six years, that was the farthest thing from my mind with what I had been through...just a feeling of emptiness way deep down inside my soul, something was really missing, and that just kept pulling at my spirit in my gut.

3

~~~

FINDING JESUS
AND A FAMILY CRISIS

One evening on May 18, 2011, I was channel surfing and I came across CTN, (Christian Television N etwork), and I saw Dr. Rodney Howard-Browne laying hands on people, they were speaking in tongues and being set free and healed of depression and illnesses in their bodies. I knew that the Holy Spirit was real because my grandmother used to speak in tongues (other languages.) I called the prayer line phone number immediately and said the Salvation Prayer with one of the members over the phone asking Jesus to come into my life and accepting Him as Lord and Savior of my life, and from that moment on something inside of me had changed. When I woke up the next day I felt different, my mind was renewed! I immediately went out and bought myself a Bible. The fire of God was burning deep inside my very soul, I felt different than I had ever felt before. I was never one who enjoyed reading, so I started reading the Bible for the very first time in my life and I was consumed with the Word of God and how it was coming alive as I read the scriptures that applied to my life and what I was believing in God for; and for Him to make himself real to me.

I started praying and walking the floors in my bedroom and living room *pressing in*, with my hands raised up to heaven asking God to deliver me from where I was in my life at that time, and the fire of God began to grow stronger and deeper within my soul; I had the fire of God burning on the inside of me that everyone was talking about, I became more hungry for the things of God with a spiritual appetite and I was desperately seeking Him. I did not yet have the anointing of the Holy Spirit and that was ok, I knew God would give it to me in His time so I was not concerned. I just kept *pressing in* and developing a close and very personal relationship with Jesus and the Father... I felt the presence of God so strong, it was powerful and I knew he was doing a great work inside of me and for that I was so grateful. I felt the depression leaving and I began to see everything so differently, I talked differently and I walked differently, I started to see people the way Jesus does, with a passion for the lost; I started to talk to people who I came across in my daily life and asked them if they knew Jesus. I keep of copy of the Salvation Prayer in my wallet so I can lead others to the Lord as I go about my day. When I spoke to my family and friends about what God was doing in my life they were amazed because they had never heard me talking this way before. I was always the go to girl if you wanted to have a party, not one who was talking about the things of God, so they were shocked at first.

My brother Rick was especially excited because he had been a man of God for his whole life, and when I told him about Dr. Rodney Howard-Browne on CTN, he said the hair stood up on the back of his neck, he knew exactly who he was! Dr. Rodney Howard-Browne had been to Bangor, Maine, twenty years ago he said, and that was who led him to the Lord! We were connecting spiritually as adults for the first time. I ask my brother what I should read in the Bible to get me to the next level and he told me to read the "Book of John", the "Book of Acts" and to look up the "Gifts of the Spirit", in the Bible. And as I read aloud to myself, the Word of God coming from my lips, I realized that speaking the Word aloud activates the Supernatural Power of God...and I was higher lifted up in my spirit and this my friends, will make you hungry for more!

Luke 8: verses 4-15: When a great crowd was gathered, and people were coming to Jesus from every town, he told them a story:

"A farmer went out to plant his seed. While he was planting, some seed fell by the road. People walked on the seed, and the birds ate it up. Some seed fell on a rock, and when it began to grow, it died because it had no water. Some seed fell among thorny weeds, but the weeds grew up with it and choked the good plants. And some seed fell on good ground and grew and made a hundred times more". As Jesus finished the story, he called out, "You people who can hear me, listen!" Jesus followers asked him what this story meant. Jesus said, "You have been chosen to know the secrets about the kingdom of God. But I use stories to speak to other people so that: "They will look, but they may not see. They will listen, but they may not understand.""

This is what the story means: The seed is God's message. The seed that fell beside the road is like the people who hear God's teaching, but the devil comes and takes it away from them so they cannot believe it and be saved.

The seed that fell on rock is like those who hear God's teaching and accept it gladly, but they don't allow the teaching to go deep into their lives. They believe for a while, but when trouble comes, they give up. The seed that fell among the thorny weeds is like those who hear God's teaching, but they let worries, riches and pleasures of this life keep them from growing and producing good fruit.

And the seed that fell on good ground is like those who hear God's teaching with good, honest hearts and obey it and patiently produce good fruit."

If you have a good and honest heart, and you're willing and obedient, your Supernatural Spiritual Journey will begin with your salvation as it has with me, and this is why I share my story with you. I absolutely believe it was God who was pulling at my spirit so strong that night when I stopped on the CTN Channel, it was by divine appointment. And that is indeed, when everything in my life began to change.

My brother was living in the state of Maine, where he had lived for most of his adult life after the military; we have always been very close. About three years ago, my brother had seen blood in his urine, so being concerned he went to the doctors and was diagnosed with a small mass or tumor that they found between his liver and the kidney, they told him it was likely to be cancer but a slow moving kind; in other words they did not create urgency for him get checked out any further? It didn't make sense to me because even if you have an unusual spot on your skin they remove it immediately. My brother rebuked it and decided to let nature take its course; from time to time, I would ask him questions about it and then we would get into an argument about what I thought he should do; time went on and he was happy and doing well, so we all went about our lives as usual.

Until June 6, 2011, when my brother went into the hospital to get a biopsy for some spots that showed up on his lungs. We stayed positive in our faith and said, no matter what happens we know and believe Jesus is the healer and we prayed together in agreement for him to be healed. We both understood the power of prayer and how what you say can make the difference between life and death; and we believed in his healing miracle to manifest.

My brother went back to the doctor for his test results with his friend Park, who had called me that afternoon to tell me my brother Rick was diagnosed with Metastatic Liposarcoma (cancer of the fat cells), and had been given one year to live; we were all devastated. Words cannot explain how it feels to have someone you love given such a diagnoses; and he was so far away that I couldn't run to be by his side. I immediately began calling all of the family and relatives and telling them about Rick and asking everyone to pray.

I was so thankful that I had found God because without him, I would not have been able to have the faith that the Lord was going to pull us through. Because God knows everything about us, I know that He knew what was coming and that is why he was pulling at me in my spirit to come to him and follow Jesus. It had just been six weeks prior to my brother's diagnosis that I called that prayer line to accept Jesus as my Lord and Savior.

From a distance, I was as supportive as I could be, calling my brother every single day and talking for hours a time and praying together. While he was continuing his routine, the rest of us did the same. I contacted a dear friend of mine Sharon who had also been reaching out to God and together she and I went to Vero Beach, Florida, for a Water Baptism in the ocean on June 26, 2011.

I'll never forget it. As I got into my car in Boynton Beach, Florida, and drove north to Vero Beach, Florida, it was a hard rain coming down, so I called my friend Sharon to see if it was raining up ahead which was only about 45 minutes away, she said no, so I continued. We met at her house and rode together in her car to the designated location for the baptism. We parked and as we got to the beach we were both surprised at how many people were there. In all, it was about two hundred people, half of them were there to be baptized and the other half was family and friends who were there to see their loved ones baptism in the ocean.

It was hurricane season and on this particular day, the skies were dark as far as you could see, with rain and some tornadoes being spotted out over the ocean, north and south from where we were. As everyone got signed in for their baptism and started to gather before heading to the shore line, I looked up at the sky, and it was as if God was blowing a perfectly large round opening in those clouds right before my eyes, and the sun came beaming through, it was amazing! The only place the sun was shining as far as you could see was right over the people on the beach who were there for the baptism. It was a beam of sunshine coming through the perfect round hole in the clouds shining down on us, I can still see it in my mind as clear as day. After the baptism in the ocean, I felt so happy, refreshed, renewed and clean inside and out...my friend and I strolled along the shore line for about an hour. We were among the last to leave and as we approached the car to go home it began to sprinkle, it was as if God was with us all along and held off the rain. The Bible says, all of heaven rejoices over one sinner who gives their life to Jesus. So it was a very good day!

4

~~~

THE PROMISE
OF THE HOLY SPIRIT

My Brother Rick's birthday was approaching on August 7, 2011. I remember, I sent him a funny musical card, when you opened it, it said; "Celebrate Accordionly"! And it was the "Chicken Dance Song", with an Accordion that unfolded when you opened the card. Oh did we laugh, my brother was always laughing, and he loved to have a good time. We talked for hours on the phone that night and afterword's, I went to bed and began reading the Bible as I had been doing each night so I could learn God's Word. While reading out loud, suddenly I began to weep and cry because of a scripture I had just read deeply moved me and the Bible fell out of my hand on to the floor, still weeping I got up to pick it up, laid back down and it fell out of my hand again, I got up, picked up my Bible and got back into bed and for the third time it was like someone gently smacked the Bible right out of my hand, it even broke a fingernail. I started laughing and now I was weeping, and laughing all at the same time. I got up to get my Bible again and the anointing of the Holy Spirit came upon me so strong, I began speaking in other tongues, I was so excited about it! I knew it was God and I knew he waited until my brother's birthday to anoint me with the Holy Spirit with the evidence of speaking in tongues (the heavenly language), so I would know that He was here with me and Jesus is alive in heaven. Because God is the one who gives the anointing of the Holy Spirit and Fire! The anointing was so strong; I could hardly speak in English for three days!

That same night, I called my friend Sharon who did not yet believe in the Holy Spirit in the middle of the night and left her a message as I was singing in tongues. She came over the next day, and I shared my testimony with her. I also called my brother Rick right away, I knew this was special. When God does something in your life, He always does it in perfect timing; He works with us in such a way that it is very personal to us. And it will always be a gift that I will cherish and use for all the days of my life.

Acts 1: verse 8; "But when the Holy Spirit comes upon you, you will receive power! And you will be my witnesses in every part of the world!"

To my knowledge through scripture; the anointing of the Holy Spirit is God in action on earth, by the presence of the Holy Spirit in one's life. When you are a "doer of

God's Word", He comes to abide in you and His will is done. This is God's way of giving you the tools you need to get the job done. God will give you direction and power you don't have in your own strength. When you step out in faith, you experience God's Supernatural Power and the level of the anointing on you increases. God offers us power, but that power comes through intimacy by spending time with God.

The anointing of the Holy Spirit is the heavenly language, the Spirit of God. He is God. Once you are given the anointing of the Holy Spirit you will always have it, unless God takes it away from you; you control when you want to press in. When you are down to your last ounce of strength, the Holy Spirit lifts and carries you.

John 15: verses 26-27; "I will send you the Helper" from the Father; he is the Spirit of Truth that comes from the Father. When he comes, he will tell about me, and you also must tell people about me, because you have been with me from the beginning."

If a Christian life is simply a matter of doing our best, there was no need for God to send the Holy Spirit to help us. After all, our best is our best. How do we improve on that? Since God is omniscient, as we certainly believe He is, He knows when we have done all we can do. Jesus let it be known, that God was looking for more than our best. He was looking for a life-style and attitude that superseded our best. A life-style and attitude we could never attain through our own effort...think about this. If we don't need any help, why send a helper? The promise of the Helper presupposes that we need help. The promise of the Helper was Jesus' way of tipping us off to one of the most profound truths concerning the Christian life. The quality of life Jesus expects from His followers is unattainable apart from the outside intervention of the anointing of the Holy Spirit. (By Max Lucado, from *The Wonderful Spirit Filled Life* by Charles Stanley)

Acts 2: verses 2-4; "When the day of Pentecost came, they were all together in one place. Suddenly a noise like a strong, blowing wind came from heaven and filled the whole house where they were sitting. They saw something like flames of fire that were separated and stood over each person there. They were all filled with the Holy Spirit, and they began to speak different languages' by the power the Holy Spirit was given them."

Acts 2: verses 6-8 & 11-13; "There were some religious Jews staying in Jerusalem who were from every country in the world. When they heard this noise, a crowd came together. They were all surprised, because each one heard them speaking in his own language. They were completely amazed at this. They said, look! Aren't all of these people that we hear speaking from Galilee? We are from different places, but yet we hear them telling in our own languages about the great things God has done! They were all amazed and confused asking each other what does this mean?" But others were making fun of them saying, "They have had too much wine."

Acts 2: verses 14-20; "But Peter stood up with the eleven apostles, and in a loud voice he spoke to the crowd: "My fellow Jews, and all of you in Jerusalem, listen to me. Pay attention to what I have to say. These people are not drunk, as you think; it is only nine o'clock in the morning! But Joel the prophet wrote about what is happening here today:

17; 'God says: In the last days I will pour out my Spirit on all kinds of people. Your sons and daughters will prophesy. Your young men will see visions, and your old men will dream dreams.

18; 'At that time I will pour out my Spirit also on my male slaves and female slaves, and they will prophesy.

19; 'I will show miracles in the sky and on the earth: blood, fire, and thick smoke.

20; 'The sun will become dark, the moon red as blood, before the overwhelming and glorious day of the Lord will come."

Pentecost came two thousand years ago, which means this; we are living in the last of the last days because it already started two thousand years ago!

2 Corinthians 1: verses 21-22; "Remember, God is the One who makes you and us strong in Christ. God made us his chosen people. He put his special mark on us to show that we are his, and he put his Spirit in our hearts to be a guarantee for all he has promised."

Acts 2: verses 38 & 39; "Change your hearts and lives and be baptized; each one of you, in the name of Jesus Christ for the forgiveness of your sins. And you will receive the gift of the Holy Spirit. This promise is for you, your children, and for all who are far away. It is for everyone the Lord our God calls to himself."

Romans 4: verses 1-5; "Since we have been made right with God by our faith, we have peace with God. This happened through our Lord Jesus Christ, who has brought us into that blessing of God's grace that we now enjoy. We also have joy with our troubles, because we know that these troubles produce patience. And patience produces character and character produces hope. And this hope will never disappoint us, because God has poured out his love to fill our hearts. He gave us his love through the Holy Spirit, whom God has given to us."

John 7: verses 37-39; "On the last and most important day of the feast Jesus stood up and said in a loud voice, "Let anyone who is thirsty come to me and drink. If anyone believes in me, rivers of living water will flow out from that person's heart." Jesus was talking about the Holy Spirit. The Spirit had not yet been given, because Jesus had not yet been raised to glory. But later, those who believed in Jesus would receive the Spirit."

God does not force anything on you, He gives us a free will; there are great rewards when you are obedient in your walk with God. You must spend quality time with God if you want anything He has promised you, and want it more than anything else this world has to offer... and ask Him for what you need and want. No one can give you what He can!

John 14: verses 15-17; The Promise of the Holy Spirit. "If you love me, you will obey my commands. I will ask the Father, and he will give you another helper" to be with you forever...the Spirit of truth. The world cannot accept him, because it does not see him or know him. But you know him, because he lives with you and he will be in you."

John 14: verses 26-29; "The Helper is the Holy Spirit whom the Father will send in my name. I leave you peace; my peace I give to you. I do not give it to you as the world does. So don't let your hearts be troubled or afraid. I have told you this now before it happens so when it happens you will believe."

John 16: verses 8-14; "When the Helper comes, (the Holy Spirit) he will prove to the people of the world the truth about sin, about being right with God, and about judgment. He will prove to them that sin is not believing in me. But when the Spirit of truth comes, he will lead you into all truth. He will not speak his own words, but he will speak only what he hears, and he will tell you what is to come. The Spirit of truth will bring glory to me, because he will take what I have to say and tell it to you."

Ephesians 1: verses 11-14; "In Christ we were chosen to be God's people, because from the very beginning God had decided this in keeping with his plan. And he is the one who makes everything agree with what he decides and wants. We are the first people who hoped in Christ, and we were chosen so that we would bring praise to God's glory. So it is with you. When you heard the true teaching-the Good News about your salvation-you believed in Christ. And in Christ, God put his special mark of ownership on you by giving you the Holy Spirit that he had promised. That Holy Spirit is the guarantee that we will receive what God promised for his people until God gives full freedom to those who are his...to bring praise to God's glory."

Ephesians 1: verses 19-21; "And you will know that God's power is very great for us who believe. That power is the same as the great strength God used to raise Christ from the dead and put him at his right side in the heavenly world. God has put Christ over all rulers, authorities, powers and kings, not only in this world but also in the next."

Acts 1: verse 3; "After Jesus death, he showed himself to them and proved in many ways that he was alive. The apostles saw Jesus during the forty days after he was raised from the dead, and he spoke to them about the kingdom of God."

The world today is looking for something real. It is tired of counterfeit spiritually empty words, lifeless formulas that don't really work, and just going through the motions. As a believer in Christ, the Holy Spirit will give you what you're really looking for!

Luke 11: verse 13; "Your heavenly Father will give the Holy Spirit to those who ask him."

The Holy Spirit has changed my life forever and he will change yours too, if you just obey God's Word and ask Him to give you the anointing of the Holy Spirit with the evidence of speaking in tongues, you will come to depend upon it just as I have. God planned that the Holy Spirit would come to empower believers! Noting in this world can give you what he can!

The Word of God and the name of Jesus and the anointing of the Holy Spirit, are all <u>weapons</u> for you to use in your daily lives! Over nine hundred million people are speaking in tongues today!

5

~~~

THE GIFT OF PROPHESY

Anyone who has the anointing enjoys having the power of the Holy Spirit in their life; our weaknesses attract God's strength and power bringing us from victory to victory when we seek him. And then I started to prophecy! Glory to God, I did not even know what this was, at certain times when I was pressing in speaking in other tongues, I could understand what the Holy Spirit was saying in English, out of my mouth. I began to prophecy over my life! I *pressed in* every day and every night because I wanted to hear what the Holy Spirit had to say; I began to depend on the Holy Spirit. I started to keep a journal and documented the dates and the things I was prophesying through the Holy Spirit because there were too many to remember over a period of time.

Acts 2: verses 17-20; "God says: In the last days I will pour out my Spirit on all kinds of people. **Your sons**

and daughter will prophesy. Your young men will see visions, and your old men will dream dreams. I will show miracles in the sky and on the earth: blood fire and thick smoke. The sun will become dark, the moon red as blood, before the overwhelming and glorious day of the Lord will come."

When you need a breakthrough in your life, it comes with precision from a word by the grace of God (prophesy), when you are seeking Him through the precious life changing powerful fellowship of the anointing of the Holy Spirit!

As fear tried to set in, my brother and I stayed strong in our faith, doing what the doctor's had said and believing in a healing miracle from Jesus. Rick began to receive treatment with Chemo Therapy at the VA Hospital in Bangor, and we discussed the option of him moving home to Tennessee so he would be near the family for support. It was such a struggle for him; he didn't want to leave the house he had just purchased two years prior with his garden and his kitties. But eventually he decided to rent out his house and come home to Tennessee in December of 2011, where we would all be together during the holidays, and where he would be close enough to me in South Florida to come and stay if he wanted to. He was always cooking as usual and in good spirits, we were all amazed with the energy he had and with his tradition of giving all his wonderful and delightful homemade cookies, pies, fudge and caramel pecan brittle that we looked forward to year after year.

After the holidays I returned back home to Florida as hard as it was to leave, I had to. My brother was not too happy with the VA Hospital in Nashville and felt very alone, not really getting the support he needed with family drama and negativity all around him and me living in South Florida. I wanted to just drop everything in my life and run to be with him, but being single and unemployed after my car accident with injuries and with limited finances, the sad truth is I couldn't. By the end of February 2012, he secretly decided to move back to Maine without telling anyone, he fled in the middle of the night; and he was not taking any phone calls or seeing anyone prior to this, I was desperately praying and pressing in for a miracle every day and night.

No one heard from him or could get a hold of him for two months, and on my birthday April 2, 2012, I received a very emotional phone call from my brother, asking me to forgive him. Ten months after his diagnosis, I began to think he had stopped his Chemo treatments and without him saying so, I knew he was not doing well. He was so strong, he never once complained or told me what was happening to him with regards to his health; I would ask, but he would never be specific because he was trying to protect me and he didn't want me to know how bad it really was, heartbreaking. And when he told me his cats would lay in bed with him and cry; I knew that they knew he was declining...tears flowing as I write these words.

During the month of May 2012, I documented many things that I prophesied through the Holy Spirit, as I was talking to God and praying on a daily basis, sometimes for many hours at a time; I will share a few of them with you. On May 14, 2012, I prophesied this: **"Behold; Ricky is to live a new, and for all of heaven he will see and to rejoice!"** So, I knew he would not be healed; he would go home to heaven where he would have eternal life forever.

Pressing into the Holy Spirit, I also prophesied this: **"He wishes to see heaven, he wants to come home, and he comes home soon."**

One day on May 24, 2012, I was walking into my living room and I began to speak to God boldly out loud, I confronted him; I told him I was ready for a change, I said; "God, I know it gets better than this!!!" And I said; "Please reveal yourself to me and your plans for me!" I was quiet for a few minutes, and then I sat down on my couch and opened my mouth to *press* into the Holy Spirit and I prophesied this: **"In fourteen days"**, the Holy Spirit said it three times, but with my mouth, he said; **"In fourteen days"**, **"In fourteen days, you will know it when you see it, open your eyes and you will see!"** So I looked at the calendar and wrote down the date, fourteen days from May 24, 2012, was going to be on June 7, 2012. I called my brother Rick, my twin sisters Rhonda and Becky and my niece Heidi, and told them what I had prophesied about and I documented it in my journal. I didn't know what was going to happen or where, but I knew something was!

Over the next week, after speaking to my brother and begging him to put my name on his medical list, which I had asked for on several occasions over the years, he had fought for the longest time, because he was just really trying to protect us all from suffering any more than we had to, he said OK; if you think you can handle it. I wanted to speak to the doctor's, he finally did it, and when I called to get a health report it was hard to swallow. The tumor had grown to be eight inches long and eight inches wide, and it was protruding down into his liver, and up into his lungs and pressing on his spine.

I was talking with Rick on the phone at the hospital and he told me, I can't do this anymore, and I could hear his pain in his voice. Trying to stay strong and calm, I told him I was coming. I used my rent money and I immediately got on a plane to Bangor, Maine so I could be with my brother. I had to be with him at any cost, it had to be me, and I wanted to be with my brother, we were always so close, and he was alone and single. I took the earliest flight I could get and while I was on the plane early morning, looking through the window into the sky, I could still see the moon and I heard the Holy Spirit say out my mouth: **"Over the Sea and Over the Sun"**. But I didn't know what it meant. And I had prophesied this on several other different occasions when I *pressed* into the Holy Spirit months prior to this time. I arrived in Bangor, Maine on June 5, 2012; Rick's Pastor's wife, Charlene picked me up at the airport and took me to the hospital where he was. It was heart wrenching and painful to see his condition, all though he was fine in his mind, he knew everything and he could communicate and he knew I was there. They had to give him so much medication for the pain that he would go in and out of a deep sleep state.

That night, I slept with him lying by his side to comfort him through the night. The next day, I just sobbed off and on all day long, no words of my own can explain my sadness or the sounds of grief and mourning that came out from the very deepest part of my soul... sounds I had never heard, coming from within my broken spirit... and at the end of the day, as my dear sweet brother started slipping away...I could not watch.

I held Rick in my arms, with my face between his shoulder and his ear and sang softly to him the song, "Fly to Jesus", we both loved that song and I told him not to be afraid, Jesus is waiting and everyone is waiting in heaven for you, mom, dad, grandma; and I ask him to promise me he would communicate with me from heaven. I didn't plan on asking him that, it just came out of my spirit. It was just him and I in the room, the nurses were stepping in and out to give me privacy, and I felt two hands lay upon my shoulder's as my face was still buried into my brothers neck, softly singing and I felt a kiss on the back of my head. The nurse came in and said, honey he's gone...I rose up and gently closed his eyes with a stern calmness over me I cannot explain...I was in shock.

My brother passed away on June 6, 2012, exactly one year to the date of his diagnosis at 5:18 p.m. that afternoon. My cell phone and the room phone rang back to back at the same time, on one line was my sister Becky and the other was my niece Heidi. They both said, they just knew.

6

~~~

MIRACLES SIGNS AND WONDERS

The nurses gave me privacy and still in shock, I looked around the room with my eyes, deep in sadness, I began to gather a few of my things a little at a time putting them in my suitcase; I began to *press* into the Holy Spirit like I always do on a daily basis and this is what came out of my mouth: **"Ricky is waving at you," and he said; "He wishes you were here!"** I couldn't believe what I had just heard! I started to cry and laugh and threw my hands up to heaven and started praising God, it was so wonderful! I ran out of the room to get my brothers friend Park, who was standing at the Nurse Station, to tell him what had just happened. I carried on about that for what seemed like five minutes just rejoicing! When I calmed down, I began to gather my things again putting them in my suitcase, and I *pressed* into the Holy Spirit and this time here is what came out of my mouth:

"He said, I went Over the Sea and Over the Sun;"
"Wave to me, when you look up at the Sun!"

Oh my God!!! I could not believe it, and the way I said it was exactly how he would say it! I smiled and cried and worshiped the Lord, I could vision it in my mind, and I knew he was in heaven, where he lives for eternal life forever and that I would see him again some sweet day!

I had an enormous amount of peace in my heart as I left that room; on my way out a nurse said to me, I'm sorry for your loss. I looked at her and said; "Thank you, he's in heaven...as I smiled;" "He is in a much better place than we are." And she said wow; I wish everyone had that attitude. I told all the nurses at the Nurse's Station and Rick's doctor what had happened and they looked at me with amazement on their faces.

My brother's friend and "Personal Assistant" took me to a quaint little Hotel nearby, like something you would see up in the Smoky Mountains, where I would spend the night alone with my Toy Pomeranian "Nigel"; he had been with me the whole time in Rick's room. The General Manager of the hotel was so kind; she brought me dinner that night, from her home where she lived up above the hotel.

As I got settled in, I began to call my family and tell them what had come out of my mouth through the Holy Spirit before I left Ricks room. I wanted to comfort them the way the Holy Spirit had comforted me, and so I shared my testimony with them all.

That night as I lay in bed all alone in a town I did not know, and without my brother, I sobbed for hours, curled up in a fetal position in the middle of the bed, my heart was completely broken into a million pieces. With visions of my brother still in my head...I just began to pray.

I was emotionally overwhelmed and exhausted, but rejoicing and deeply grieving, all at the same time. The presence of God was so strong around me, it was God who sustained me, and He gave me such peace and a wonderful miracle, like one I had never heard of before. And it was at this time that I understood; my brother did not want to be healed. He wanted to go to heaven since he was seven, because that's when our mom went home to heaven. He was tired of the struggles he had endured all throughout his life. Now his struggle was over, and he is a "new man" living eternal life in heaven. Glory to God who gives us victory through His Son Christ Jesus!

James 4: verse 2; "You have not, because you have not asked me!"

Luke 1: verse 37; "For with God nothing is impossible!"

The next morning on June 7, 2012, my brother's friend took me to the Bangor airport to catch a flight home to Nashville, Tennessee; where we would have my brother's memorial. I arrived in Nashville around 5:00 p.m. My sister Becky picked me up at the airport and we headed back to her house in Antioch, Tennessee. As we pulled into the driveway my other sister Rhonda came out to greet me as we got out of the car; then the three of us continued to walk on towards the front of the house and I said to the girls, remember what the Holy Spirit said about Rick; **"He said, I went Over the Sea and Over the Sun"**... **"Wave to me, when you look up at the sun!"** and I said, "lets blow him a kiss", and all three of us blew him and kiss and waved up at the sun; and all of a sudden the sun began flashing at us! Rhonda noticed it first because she was behind me, and said, look Carol! The sun is flashing at us! We all looked and began walking in amazement onto the grass and the sun was flashing! And it started spinning all at the same time! **It was a "Supernatural Encounter with God!" And suddenly, I realized it was what I had prophesied about on May 24, 2012!** I looked at the girls and I said; it's June 7, 2012; remember what I told you about, **"it's been fourteen days, and this is it!"** My body was shaking all over under the power of God, and I began to realize at that moment, that God waited until I was with my two twin sisters, so they would believe and have faith and to give them peace, so they knew He was real and Jesus was alive in heaven, and our brother Rick was alive and in heaven too! My eyes could not look away, I held my hands up to the sky to worship, not sure of how long this Supernatural Encounter with God, "Miracles in the Sky" would last; it had already been about ten minutes so the glow of colors around the sun had already passed, and my sister Becky got my cell phone/camera out my purse that I had dropped to the ground, and she began snapping photos, one after another. God was moving so fast in my life at that time, I could not keep up with Him! Glory to God, Hallelujah!

It was at the end of the day, so the sun was going down around 6:30 p.m., it lasted for thirty minutes, the sun was flashing and spinning like a strobe light all at the same time; at first a light pastel glow of colors would appear around the sun that would change from orange, to red, to purple while this was all happening! During this thirty minutes of our glorious Supernatural Encounter with God of Miracles in the sky, the clouds began shifting around until they formed into the shape of a Cross right before our very eyes! And then, behind the Cross of Clouds you could see the face of our Lord Jesus Christ!

So many phenomenal things are taking place at the same time in these photographs. You can also see what looks like a Red Bubble with a light on the inside of it, as it gets closer and closer to us, the color of it also gets more bold. I believe this is my Brother Rick's Spirit; however we could not see it with the naked eye, this is referred to as an Orb, which is believed to be the true form of spirit or souls. (*Not referring to the Spirit Orb as Biblical Prophecy*).

In this book, is the first time I have ever shared any of these photographs with the public, unless it was a close friend or family member and when I was sharing my testimony with someone to lead them to the Lord; **because it is Holy**!

I have twenty one photographs that were taken on June 7, 2012, by my sister Becky in front of her house with my cell phone/camera; and the following are seven of the best photos that I have selected for your viewing, of the day that God Almighty revealed himself to us in the sky; this is what I had prophesied about fourteen days before it happened...**a Supernatural Encounter with God in the sky, is a Miracle, a Sign and a Wonder!**

(This is one of the Scriptures that make these miracles Biblically Prophetic.)

Acts 2: verses 17-21: God says: "in the last days" **"I will pour out my spirit on all flesh**, (The Holy Spirit). **Your sons and daughters will prophesy**. Your young men will see visions, and your old men will dream dreams. **I will show miracles in the sky and on the earth**: blood, fire, and thick smoke. The sun will become dark, the moon red as blood, before the overwhelming and glorious day of the Lord will come."

This is something only God can do! A Supernatural Encounter with God that is Biblically Prophetic is meant for the whole world to know about, to show God's glory and for lost souls to be saved for the kingdom of heaven before Jesus Christ comes again...because the End of time is near!

Photo One – After the three of us waived up at the sun and blew my brother a kiss, the sun starting flashing at us, then it was flashing and spinning like a strobe light all at the same time! By the time my sister Becky thought to get my cell phone/camera out of my purse that I had dropped on the ground, the light pastel glow of colors around the sun had already passed.

Photo Two – This is me in the photograph, I could not move; my body was shaking all over as I lifted my hands up to the sky praising God. It was not until much later, as I looked at these photographs many times...did I notice the Red Spirit Orb directly above the sun. As you can imagine, these photographs cannot even compare to having the experience of this "Supernatural Encounter with God in the sky", that I also prophesied about fourteen days before it happened! (*Not saying the Spirit Orb is Biblically Prophetic*)

Photo Three – While the Sun was still flashing and spinning like a strobe light; looking at the photos you can see what looks like the image of a face starting to form in the clouds to the left of the sun. But, we did not realize it at the time because we were watching the sun; notice the Spirit Orb that was directly above the sun has changed positions as it gets closer and closer. It was all a phenomenal, profound unique miracle that we were being a part of, and it is another fulfillment of Biblical Prophecy of miracles in the sky! (*Not referring to the Spirit Orb as Biblical Prophecy*).

Photo Four – Fifteen minutes later the sun was still flashing and spinning, stronger than ever; we were having a "Supernatural Encounter with God in the sky!" Notice the image in the clouds to the left of the sun starting to form, and you can also clearly see how the Spirit Orb gets closer and bolder in color each time. But remember, it's all about Jesus and Biblical Prophecy and the Supernatural Power of God Almighty! (Not referring to the Spirit Orb as Biblical Prophecy).

Photo Five – Twenty minutes later the sun was still flashing and spinning; this is also when the clouds started to shift around right before our very eyes! You can see how the Spirit Orb is now right in front of us; however we could not see it with the naked eye. (Not referring to the Spirit Orb as Biblical Prophecy). IT'S ALL ABOUT JESUS!

Photo Six – After thirty minutes the sun became calm again, and the clouds shifting had formed into the shape of a cross. Then we could clearly see the Cross of Clouds and the face of Jesus behind the cross! (Look at the top left of this photo, find the cross of clouds and look for his eyes above where the cross meets, see the whites of his eyes, his eye brows and hair; some say it looks like the crown of thorns.) Try to imagine how enormous this profound miracle was to us in the sky by comparing it to the land. Glory, glory, glory! Hallelujah! Thank you Father God Almighty!

Photo Seven - This Supernatural Encounter with God of miracles in the sky has been the "Burning Bush" in my life! (**Exodus 3: 1-4 & 4:23;** "When God spoke to Moses, using a Burning Bush to get Moses attention.") It's all about Jesus! This is a closer view slightly enlarged of photo six; with the Cross of Clouds and the face of Jesus! This is the "Supernatural Power of God!" It is a very profound, unique miracle in the sky, and it is from Heaven! *Glory to God Hallelujah!!*

This is something only GOD can do! We are all precious in the eyes of the Lord; this is all about our next life, eternal life in heaven through our Lord Jesus Christ!

There is no doubt that these unique, profound miracles are all from heaven; in these photographs God is displaying His Glory and Supernatural Power with miracles in the sky just like he said he would in His Word! It may have never happened if I hadn't asked. That's why we shouldn't put limits on God, nothing is impossible with Him! I feel so blessed and honored to have experienced such profound and beautiful, phenomenal, unique miracles from heaven; it has changed my life forever!

Mark 5: verse 19; "Go home to your family and tell them how much the Lord has done for you and how he has had mercy on you."

We can do nothing without God, and until our hearts are ready to let Him use us, He cannot perform miracles through us! Submit your heart to the Lord and you will see His divine favor and excessive blessings! God is moving by His Spirit all over the earth with great miracles, signs and wonders...and it will be the anointing of God that will protect His people in this last hour. God is calling people higher, and the focus is on eternity!

Hebrews 4: verse 16; "Let us then, feel very sure that we can come boldly before God's Throne where there is grace. There we can receive mercy and grace to help us when we need it."

It is by faith that I came boldly to the Throne of God and asked him to reveal himself and his plans for me in my living room that day on May 24, 2012, and He answered me back! It pleases God when He knows we believe in Him and stand on His Word and proclaim it, regardless of what the circumstances are around us! That's when you see your miracles happen!

Job 5: verse 9; "God does wonder's that cannot be understood; he does so many miracles they cannot be counted."

God meets you at the level of your expectation! When you have "Now Faith" and go through your day with expectancy, you'll see God show up in amazing ways!

It's God's passionate desire to bless you! His greatest glory is to bring joy, love and peace to all who become a part of His kingdom! And when you let Jesus come into your life you will see His Supernatural Favor!

2 Chronicles 16: verse 9; "For the eyes of the Lord run to and fro throughout the whole earth, to show himself strong on behalf of those whose **heart** is loyal to him."

Jesus says in John 14: verse 21; "He who has my commandments and keeps them, it is he who loves me. And he who loves me will be loved by my Father, and I will love him and **manifest (show)** myself to him."

God knew how much we needed Him, after so much tragedy and loss in our family lives; He gave us victory over death. I am no longer afraid to die or afraid for anyone else to die, because I know I am going home to heaven and so are all of those who believe and obey God's Word. Heaven is real and Jesus is alive and for all who believe that Jesus Christ is their Lord and Savior, will also have eternal life in heaven for ever more! It is very clear that my brother Rick did not want to be healed by Jesus; he was ready to go home to Heaven, as he had wanted since he was seven years old.

1 Corinthians 2: verses 9-10; "No eye has seen, nor ear has heard, and no mind has imagined what God has prepared for those who love Him." "But God has shown us these things through the Spirit. For His Spirit searches out everything, and shows us God's deep secrets."

As believers, God's Spirit lives on the inside of us, revealing to us the heart and thoughts of God Himself. I am eternally grateful for the Love of God and our Lord Jesus Christ and the precious life changing fellowship of the Holy Spirit and the gift of prophecy. Without them all, I wouldn't be where I am today and I would have never had these phenomenal unique miracles in my life that I share with you today!

I want to encourage you to ask God for the anointing of the Holy Spirit with the evidence of speaking in tongues, and let revival come into every area of your life too! The anointing of the Holy Spirit is given to everyone who is hungry for Him, and the excessive blessings of God are visible! When you are obedient in your walk with God, you will have breakthrough after breakthrough!

He will change you by bringing you from glory to glory! As a "Born Again Believer" your transformation should continue and it is progressive! When people see you, they should see Jesus in your eyes, hear him in your voice, and feel him in your touch.

The anointing of the "Holy Spirit" and the "Fire of God" gives you the Supernatural Power to do what you cannot do in the natural!

1 Corinthians 12: verses 7-11; "Gifts from the Holy Spirit" something from the Spirit can be seen in each person, for the common good. The Spirit gives one person the ability to speak with wisdom, and the same Spirit gives another the ability to speak with knowledge. The same Spirit gives faith to one person. And, to another, that one Spirit gives gifts of healing. The Spirit gives another person the power to do miracles, to another the ability to prophesy. And he gives to another the ability to know the difference between good and evil spirits. The Spirit gives one person the ability to speak in different kinds of languages" and to another the ability to interpret those languages. One Spirit, the same Spirit, does all these things, and the Spirit decides what to give to each person."

When you accept Jesus as your Lord and Savior; you have the most powerful source of the Universe on the inside of you; there is strength, there is victory, there is discipline, and there is favor when you have Jesus in your life. It is a great privilege that we can ask God for something and He will give it to us!

God is looking for those who are "Doers of the Word" that he can lift up and favor and be blessed!

Don't ever, criticize the move of the Lord; it is HOLY!

Romans 8: verses 31 & 38-39; "If God is with us, no one can defeat us." "Yes, I am sure that neither death, nor life, nor angels, nor ruling spirits, nothing now, nothing in the future, no powers, nothing above us, nothing below us, nor anything else in the whole world will ever be able to separate us from the love of God that is in Christ Jesus our Lord."

James 1: verses 17-18; "Every good action and every perfect gift is from God. These good gifts come down from the Creator of the Sun, the Moon and the Stars! God decided to give us life through The Word of Truth so we might be the most important of all the things he made."

Matthew 12: verses 30-32; "Whoever is not with me is against me. Whoever does not work with me is working against me. "I tell you the truth, all sins that people do and all things people say against God can be forgiven. But whoever speaks against the **Holy Spirit** will not be forgiven; he is guilty of sin that continues for ever. Anyone who speaks against the Son of man can be forgiven, but anyone who speaks against the Holy Spirit will not be forgiven, now or in the future.

Psalms 107: verse 20; "He sent His Word and healed them, and delivered them from their destructions."

God sent His Word to heal and deliver us. The Father sent Jesus, not only to save us from our sins, but also to heal our bodies. **John 19: verse 30**; "On the cross Jesus said; "It is finished" then he bowed his head and died." It was not only your sin that was removed, but also your sickness and disease. All throughout the Bible, Jesus healed everywhere he went and there was a glorious display of God's Supernatural Power; and his followers would share the Good News!

Hebrews 13: verse 8; "Jesus is the same yesterday, today and forever!"

He is still healing millions of people every day and night all over the world!

1 Peter 2: verses 24-25; "By his stripes you are healed!" "Christ carried our sins in his body to the cross so we would stop living for sin. And you are healed because of his wounds." **Jesus stripes** are the **39** lashes he had on his body when he died for us on the cross.

Jesus Christ performed mass miracles by the power of his Father God; people would come from miles around into cities and towns when they heard where Jesus would be, with their sick loved ones to be healed. Multitudes of healing sickness and distressing bodily plagues and evil spirits, and many who were blind he gave (a free, gracious, joy-giving gift of sight!) People would praise the Lord with amazement because of his power and his love for all. He turned water into wine at a wedding in Galilee, he walked on the water and stood waiting for his followers who would soon arrive in their boat, he fed five thousand people with five loafs of bread and two fish (that never ran out); he healed the paralyzed and crippled, and raised people from the dead! He would teach Gods Word and truths and what was to come including the Holy Spirit. In the "Book of Acts, Matthew, Mark, Luke and John" in the Bible; multitudes of healing miracles took place and continued to take place after Jesus went home to heaven to be with the Father God; these miracles would still continue all throughout the world as Jesus promised, and they are still taking place today. The Spirit of Jesus always comes when we call upon His name for anything that we might need. Literally anything, you and I need!

Mark 16: verses 16-20; "Anyone who believes and is baptized will be saved, but anyone who does not believe will be punished. And those who believe will be able to do these things as proof: They will use my name to force out demons. "They will speak in new languages." They will pick up snakes and drink poison without being hurt. "They will touch the sick, and the sick will be healed." After the Lord Jesus said these things to his followers, he was carried up into heaven, and he sat at the right side of God. The followers went everywhere in the world and told the Good News to people, and the Lord helped them. The Lord proved that the Good News they told was true by giving them power to work miracles."

The reason God gets upset about sin, is because it allows evil spirits to enter into our lives, and the thing that really makes God mad is Unbelief! Because that will steal all the miracles and blessings that God wants to give you! So when you read the Bible; read it like you believe it and take it literally!

John 14: verses 1-4; Jesus said "Don't let your hearts be troubled. Trust in God, and trust in me. There are many rooms in my Father's house; I would not tell you this if it were not true. I am going there to prepare a place for you. After I go and prepare a place for you, I will come back and take you to be with me so that you may be where I am. You know the way to the place where I am going."

John 14: verse 12; "I tell you the truth, anyone who believes in me will do the same works I have done, and even greater works, because I am going home to be with the Father."

Jesus is declaring an amazing truth. We will do miracles, even greater than he has done! Truth of Jesus teaching is not merely a comforting idea, or pious meditation. Jesus taught these principles as a reality to be experienced by anyone who would truly listen to and believe what he was saying!

In the Bible, Paul says that "in the ages to come" God would do things that would exceed anything He has ever done before!

I believe that "the ages to come" is this day and time we are living in right now! God wants to outdo Himself in our generation, because the "end of time is near!"

7

≈

SALVATION

Hebrews 2: verses 2-4; Our Salvation is great! "So we must be more careful to follow what we are taught. Then we will not stray away from the truth. The Lord himself first told about this salvation, and it was proven true to us by those who heard him. God also proved it by using wonders, great signs, many kinds of miracles, and by giving people gifts through the Holy Spirit, just as he wanted."

John 14: verses 6-7; Jesus said, "I am the way, and the truth, and the life. The only way to the Father is through me."

There's only one way to get to God, and that's through Jesus!

God uses ordinary people just like you and me. All you have to do is **seek Him**, and begin to develop an intimate relationship with God and with Jesus and the fellowship of the Holy Spirit. He gives us a choice to have a new life with our salvation, you are forgiven of all sin, you are born again, and you are washed by the blood of Jesus; your salvation is signed, sealed and delivered! Either you are a doer of the Word of God or you are not! You can't have it both ways!

2 Corinthians 4: verses 3-6; "If the Good News that we preach is hidden, it is hidden only to those who are lost. The devil who rules this world has blinded the minds of those who do not believe. They cannot see the light of the Good News...The Good News about the glory of Christ, who is exactly like God. We do not preach about ourselves, but we preach that Jesus Christ is Lord and that we are your servants for Jesus. God once said, "Let the light shine out of the darkness!" This is the same God who made his light shine in our hearts by letting us know the glory of God that is in the face of Christ.

2 Corinthians 4: verses 13-15; "It is written in the Scriptures, "I believed, so I spoke." Our faith is like this too. We believe, and so we speak. God raised the Lord Jesus from the dead, and we know that God will also raise us with Jesus. God will bring us together with you, and we will stand before him. All these things are for you. And so the grace of God that is being given to more and more people will bring increasing thanks to God for his glory."

The best decision you could ever make in your lifetime and for your families lives, is to surrender your life to God and follow Jesus. With Him all things are possible. In the day and times that we live in now, "The End Times", people of the world are desperate and they need to have God in their lives to survive!

2 Corinthians 5: verse 10; "because we must stand before Christ to be judged. Each one of us will receive what we should get...good or bad...for the things we did in the earthly body."

The incredible events which have taken place in our nation have left many people paralyzed with fear, and spreading fear was the very purpose of these hideous deeds, which were master-mined by Satan himself. The devil is a master at using people to do his dirty deeds, and many times convincing the perpetrators that they are actually doing something God wanted them to do. (By Max Lucado) "Be not deceived; God is not mocked..." **Galatians 6: verse 7**; "The biggest fool in the world is the fool that fools himself."

When you are saved, the supernatural power of Gods anointing comes on you to break every yoke of bondage, and stronghold off of your life. We all need God to help us in every area of our lives. When you accept Jesus as your Lord and Savior, all of heaven rejoices over that one person; and your name is written in the "Lambs Book of Life."

Romans 10: verses 9-10; "If you declare with your mouth, "Jesus is Lord," and believe in your heart that God raised him from the dead, you will be saved. For it is with your heart that you believe and are justified, and it is with your mouth that you profess your faith and are saved."

Once you believe in Jesus, you open the door for God to move into your family's life and touch every member. It is God's desire for your entire household to be saved!

Has anyone ever told you that God loves you and He has a great plan for your life? I have a real quick but important question to ask you. If you were to die this very second, do you know for sure, beyond a shadow of a doubt, that you would go to Heaven?

Let me quickly share with you what the Holy Bible reads. "For all have sinned and come short of the glory of God" and "for the wages of sin is death, but the gift of God is Eternal Life through Jesus Christ our Lord". The Bible also reads for whosoever calls upon the name of the Lord shall be saved." And you're a "Whosoever" right? Of course you are; all of us are. God loves you and has a wonderful plan for your life!

You must first say the salvation prayer that I am including here in my book, so you can stop and say it right now, hold your right hand up to heaven because this is where your help comes from, and with your heart and with your lips out loud, say the prayer and be saved. And please use this to save others you know, and lead them to the Lord. Tomorrow may never come for that person you love who is not saved; even you may never have this chance again. It is time for this nation to be shaken in every household! If you have family living with you, gather them all together at the same time and read the prayer aloud and let them repeat it after you, you'll be so glad that you did; you will see their countenance change on their faces. It is your choice to let God move in your life or not; you set the pace. It's time to do things you have not done before; we are his hands, his feet and his mouth. Thank God for the opportunity, when you love Jesus, you love people. It's not too late for God to do a miracle in your heart. ☺

~~~~~~~~~~~~~~~~~~~~~~~~~~~~~~

THE GOSPEL SOUL WINNING SCRIPTURE

Dear Lord Jesus, come into my heart. Forgive me of my sin. Wash me and cleanse me. Set me free. Jesus, thank you that you died for me. I believe that you were raised from the dead and that you live in heaven and that you are coming back again for me. Fill me with the Holy Spirit. Give me a passion for the lost, a hunger for the things of God and the Holy boldness to preach the gospel of Jesus Christ. I'm saved; I'm born again, I'm forgiven and I'm on my way to Heaven because I have Jesus in my heart. Amen

Now worship the Lord and thank Him! Praise His Holy name! Thank you Wonderful Lord Jesus!

As a minister of the gospel of Jesus Christ, I tell you today that all of your sins are forgiven. Always remember to run to God and not from God because he loves you and he has a great plan for your life. And you will never be the same again. You are anointed and empowered to be who God created you to be. Follow up with a water baptism as soon as possible.

~~~~~~~~~~~~~~~~~~~~~~~~~~~

Colossians 3: verses 10; "You have begun to live the new life, in which you are being made new and are becoming like the One who made you. This new life brings you the true knowledge of God."

1 Peter 2: verses 24-25; "Christ carried our sins in his body on the cross so we would stop living for sin and start living for what is right. And you are healed because of his wounds. You were like sheep that wandered away, but now you have come back to the Shepard and Protector of your souls."

Psalms 34: verses 17–18; "The Lord hears his people when they call to him for help. He rescues them from all their troubles. The Lord is close to the brokenhearted; He rescues those whose spirits have been crushed."

God's love is His free gift to you, and it will heal you everywhere you hurt.

Psalms 91: verse 11; "For He shall give His angels charge over you, to keep you in all your ways."

As you go about your day, know that God is lovingly watching over you, and has sent his angels before you to protect and to preserve you!

Kindly humble yourself; we are all called for such a time as this, the "End Times." We can only take people to heaven with us, not our worldly processions or money. As I look around in each room of my house, at the unopened boxes of my brother's personal belongings; I am very aware of how the material things in this life don't mean as much to me anymore. I feel a change inside of me, and the desires for the things of this world have grown strangely dim; my priorities have changed, focusing more on the eternal things of life are in the forefront of my mind these days; I have given Jesus first place in my life because I know with Him, the wind of God is always blowing on my back. And it is He who will give me the dreams and the desires of my heart.

Did you know there are still many generations in the world today who have never heard about Jesus or the Word of God! You might be the only one in that person or child's life who has ever told them about our heavenly Father God and Jesus Christ our Lord and Savior. Be thankful if you have a friend or family member who is hungry for the things of God. There are not a lot of them around. This world is in desperate need of every person to make a difference in the lives of people, in this life and for eternal life in heaven!

AMERICA NEEDS THE GOSPEL OF JESUS CHRIST! You have to be interactive with God, without His presence all you have is religion! "Jesus is the Hope of All the world and He is our only hope for glory!"

Some of you right now are in the wilderness of your life and whether you know it or not, God is working some junk out of you that needs to come out before you're going to be ready to have what He has promised you. Open your heart and re-dedicate your life to Jesus today, and allow God to help you by giving you the power to do what pleases Him, so He can do miracles through you, and let God take you to the place He wants you to be.

Proverbs 11: verse 30; "He who wins Souls is wise!"

James 5: verses 19 -20; Saving a Soul; If one of you wonders away from the truth, and someone helps that person come back, remember this: Anyone who brings a sinner back from the wrong way will save that sinner's soul from death and will cause many sins to be forgiven.

Colossians 3: verses 3-4; "Think only about the things in heaven, not the things on earth. Your old sinful self has died, and your new life is kept with Christ in God. Christ is our life and when he comes again, you will share in his glory."

All across the world, in over one hundred countries this Salvation Prayer is being used, so that people outside of the four walls of the church can be saved. Millions of people are being saved and set free from, sickness, diseases, drug and alcohol addiction, un-forgiveness, depression, jealousy, anxiety, oppression, fear, heartbreak, loneliness, sex addiction, adultery and marriages are being restored. This is the greatest Revival the world has ever seen! Whatever it is, you will be set free!

When you ask for forgiveness this is your promise to never do it again. And the power of God will literally burn everything that is unholy completely out of your body. You will feel the pure authentic move of God in your life, and you will begin to be the very best you have ever been, with a **changed heart.** A better person, a better spouse, a better worker, a better decision maker, better with whatever you do for a living and in your daily lives and for those you love....your life will be changed in every way.

8

~~~

BLOOD MOONS

God created the Sun, the Moon and the Stars. And he has used them all to give guidance to His followers in the Bible and on earth today, with great miracles and signs and wonders in the sky. He created heaven and earth and all of the things in it. God spoke_things into existence and He controls the universe! Don't even try to work it out in your mind!

God uses the Sun the Moon and the Stars to interact with mankind to get our attention.

NASA predicts the coming of the FOUR BLOOD MOONS – 'TETRAD' that line up with Biblical Scripture! This has happened three times in the last **500** years. In the year 1493-94; Fall of Spain, Jews expelled, Columbus discovers America, Year 1949-50; Follows Israel declared a nation, Year 1967-68; Six Day War.

THE NEXT FOUR BLOOD MOONS

April 15, 2014 – **Blood Moon – Jewish Passover;** / October 8, 2014 – **Blood Moon –Feast of Tabernacles;** / March 20, 2015 - **Solar Eclipse** / April 4, 2015 - **Blood Moon – Jewish Passover;** / September 28, 2015 - **Blood Moon – Feast of Tabernacles.**

God is sending planet earth signs that something big is about to happen, and it's already happening! History has now changed with the vicious "Isis Terrorist Organization" and the outbreak of "Ebola" a fast and fatal disease! More has happened since the first Lunar (Blood Moon) than in the last fifty years, and it is ALL Biblical Prophecy!

Don't be alarmed, be alert and be ready. Only God knows the day Jesus will come again...but we are running out of time, He is coming very soon!

Don't Fear

2 Timothy 1: verse 7; "God did not give us a spirit that makes us afraid but a spirit of power and love and self-control."

Luke 21: verses 25-31; "There will be signs in the sun, moon, and stars. On earth, nations will be afraid and confused because of the roar and fury of the sea. People will be so afraid they will faint, wondering what is happening to the world, because the powers of the heavens will be shaken. Then people will see the Son of man coming in a cloud with power and great glory.

When you see these things begin to happen, look up and hold your heads high, because the time when God will free you is near!"

Acts 2: verse 19; "I will show miracles in the sky and on earth: blood, fire, and thick as smoke. The sun will become dark, **the moon red as blood**, before the overwhelming and glorious day of the Lord will come."

The Rapture is the next prophetic event to happen on earth according to God's Word. **"Rapture"** is (The Beginning of the End) it's the first phase of the second coming of Jesus Christ. Over one hundred thirty million people in America believe in the Rapture.

Matthew 24: verses 3-15 & 21; "And what will be the sign that it is time for you to come again and for this age to end? Jesus answered, "Be careful that no one fools you. Many will come in my name, saying, 'I am the Christ', and they will fool many people. You will hear about war and stories of wars that are coming, but don't be afraid. These things must happen before the end comes. Nations will fight against other nations; kingdoms will fight against other kingdoms. There will be times when there is no food for people to eat, and there will be earthquakes in different places. These things are like the first pains when something new is about to be born. Then people will arrest you, hand you over to be hurt, and kill you. At that time many people will lose their faith, and they will turn against each other and hate each other. Many false prophets will come and cause people to believe lies. There will be more and more evil in the world, so most people will stop showing their love for each other. But those people who keep their faith until the end will be saved. The Good News about God's kingdom will be preached in all the world, to every nation. Then the end will come."

"Daniel the prophet spoke about 'the destroying terror'. You will see this standing in the holy place." (You who read this should understand what it means.) Because at that time there will be much trouble; There will be more trouble than there has ever been since the beginning of the world until now, and nothing as bad will ever happen again. God has decided to make that terrible time short. Otherwise, no one would go on living. But God will make that time short to help the people he has chosen."

Matthew 24: verses 27-35; "When the Son of Man comes, he will be seen by everyone, like lightning flashing from the east to the west. Wherever the dead body is, there the vultures will gather. Soon after the trouble of those days, 'the sun will grow dark, and the moon will not give its light. The stars will fall from the sky. And the powers of the heaven will be shaken." "At that time, the sign of the Son of Man will appear in the sky. Then all the people of the world will cry. They will see the Son of Man coming on the clouds in the sky with great power and glory. He will use a loud trumpet to send his angels all around the earth, and they will gather his chosen people from every part of the world."

"Learn a lesson from the fig tree: When its branches become green and soft and new leaves appear, you know summer is near. "In the same way, when you see all these things happening, you will know that the time is near, ready to come. I tell you the truth, all these things will happen while the people of this time are still living. Earth and sky will be destroyed, but the words I have said will never be destroyed."

Joel 3: verses 15-17; "The sun and the moon will become dark, and the stars will stop shining. The Lord will roar like a lion from Jerusalem; his loud voice will thunder from that city, and the sky and the earth will shake. But the Lord will be a safe place for his people, a strong place of safety for the people of Israel (believers). Then you will know that I am Lord you're God, alive on my holy mountain Zion."

Mark 13: verses 24-26; "During the days after this trouble comes, the sun will grow dark, and the moon will not give its light. The stars will fall from the sky. And the powers of the heavens will be shaken. Then the people will see the Son of Man coming in the clouds with great power and glory. Then he will send his angels all around the earth to gather his chosen people from every part of the earth and from every part of heaven."

God says when you see these signs, lift up your head and rejoice because the Lord Jesus is coming soon! If you are a believer in Christ Jesus and you have been saved, you are sheltered in the arms of God. We shall rejoice in knowing that we have eternal life together in heaven forever, where there is no more evil, war, sadness, sickness, pain or tears.

Equip yourselves for what is coming!

Only those worthy of being saved will be spared Tribulation.

Revelations; the last book in the Bible tells us what is coming very soon! Our time is running out! You won't be able to escape the destruction! The End of Time Is Near!

Psalm 91: verses 1-8; "Those who go to God Most High for safety will be protected by the Almighty. I will say to the Lord, "You are my place of safety and protection. You are my God and I trust you." God will save you from hidden traps and from deadly diseases. He will cover you with his feathers, and under his wings you can hide. His truth will be your shield and protection. You will not fear any danger by night or an arrow during the day. You will not be afraid of diseases that come in the dark or sickness that strikes at noon. At your side one thousand people may die, or even ten thousand right beside you, but you will not be hurt. You will only watch and see the wicked punished."

Are you prepared to die? If you are not a believer in Jesus Christ or if you have sinned against God's commands, you will be separated from God for all eternity. Re-dedicate your life to Jesus, repent of your sins and turn to Jesus Christ for your salvation today!

9

~~~

OBEDIENCE

We are born with the seed planted in us for God's Holy vision. One thing God looks for in every generation is for someone to Obey His Word and to do what He tells them to do; it's the will of God that we do this, because outside of Jesus everything will eventually fail.

1 John 5: verses 1-5; "Everyone who believes that Jesus is the Christ is God's child, and whoever loves the Father also loves the Father's children. This is how we know we love God's children: when we love God and obey his commands. Loving God means obeying his commands. And God's commands are not too hard for us, because everyone who is a child of God conquers the world. And this is the victory that conquers the world...our faith. So the one who wins against the world is the person who believes that Jesus is the Son of God."

When you want what you've never had, you need to do what you've never done. Nothing is impossible to those who believe in a God that never fails! Get Plugged-In to God and give Him something to work with! Faith without works is nothing!

Proverbs 16: verse 20; "Whoever listens to what is taught will succeed, and whoever trusts the Lord will be happy." "Those who listen to instruction will prosper!"

When you are saved, The Glory of God is always within you, He gives you His DNA, you have been given "Dominion" the two keys are (Authority & Power) given to you by God to speak His Word over your life so it can manifest, and come to pass. Why do we settle for less when we all have so much potential; you need to make it a habit and exercise the Authority and Power He has given you in your daily lives if you want to have a victorious life!

Grab ahold of your "Dominion" from God and take control! Don't let mistakes of the past keep you captive, change your mind. God wants your situation to change as much as you want it to change. Speak to your mountain and God will do what He promised He would do. Break through poverty with success. With God's divine favor on your life there is nothing you cannot do greater than you've ever done it before. Ask GOD for what you need and be specific, and have absolute trust in Him!

Always praise God, and the Lord Jesus Christ, in good times and in bad. He knows all about your struggles. He knows the burdens you carry, and the concerns of your heart, and He cares for you.

Philippians 2: verses 12-13; "My dear friends, you have always obeyed God when I was with you. It is even more important that you obey God while I am away from you. Keep on working to complete your salvation with fear and trembling, because God is working in you to help you, giving you the power to do what pleases him."

Supernatural Financial Provision and Obligating God; God challenges us to obey His Word. He even says, **"Prove Me!"**(Malachi 3:10). "Bring to the storehouse a full tenth of what you earn, so there will be food in my house." "I will open the windows of heaven for you and pour out all the blessings you need!"

What God is referring to here, is your Tithe. We are required to Tithe a Ten Percent offering of our earnings into the ministry that you attend or the ministry that blesses you and feeds your spirit and teaches you the truth of God's Word, whether in person or on TV or by the World Wide Web. Tithe, is giving to honor God. Don't come empty handed, give Him something to work with! What he has is far greater than what you and I have!

Leviticus 27: verse 30; "And all the tithe of the land, whether the seed of the land or the fruit of the tree, is the Lord's. It is Holy to the Lord."

Everything we have has been given to us by God. He has entrusted us with His resources and wants us to be good stewards of what we have. How do we increase what we have? By sowing, and giving and by being faithful and obedient to Him. Just like planting a seed in the natural yields a harvest of increase, when you sow finances to God's work, you'll receive an abundant harvest in return.

Remember, God wants to bless you excessively. He wants to increase you. When you give, when you sow, when you honor Him with your first fruits, that's when you'll see the windows of heaven open. That's when you'll see His hand of provision and excessive blessings in your life. Give back to God, be a faithful steward, and He will give back to you!

Luke 16: verses 10-12; "Whoever can be trusted with a little can also be trusted with a lot, and whoever is dishonest with a little is dishonest with a lot." "If you cannot be trusted with worldly riches, then who will trust you with true riches?" "And if you cannot be trusted with things that belong to someone else, who will give you things of your own?"

Sowing seed in a time of famine is a powerful demonstration of your faith and gives God a mighty opportunity to prove Himself strong on your behalf, that you will turn out to be a sign and a wonder to those who do not believe. God will bless you because He loves you and at the same time, He will show His glory through you to those who have not yet bowed their knee. Some people don't believe that you can trust God for a 100-fold return on your giving, but Jesus talked about it several times.

Who in their right mind wouldn't want that; and he tells us how to get it! It's all about trust; He will make the ninety percent go a lot further! There is nothing that

God tells us to do that's for him, he does it for us so we can have a more abundant life and with overflowing joy and excessive blessings the way God planned it to be! So when you read the Bible, read it like you believe it, and take it literally by being obedient and doing what God's Word says!

Luke 6: verse 38; "Give and you shall receive." "You will be given much. Pressed down, and shaken together and running over, it will spill into your lap. The way you give to others is the way God will give to you."

Job 36: verse 11; "If they listen and obey God, then they will be blessed with prosperity."

Joshua 1: verses 8-9; "Always remember that it is written in the book of teachings (Bible) study it day and night to be sure to **obey** everything that is written there. If you do this, you will be wise and successful in everything. Remember that I commanded you to be strong and brave. Don't be afraid, because the Lord your God will be with you everywhere you go."

Deuteronomy 8: verses 17-18; "You might say to yourself, I am rich because of my own power and strength, but remember the Lord your God! It is He who gives you the power to become rich, keeping the agreement He promised to your ancestors, as it is today."

Matthew 6: verses 33-34; "The thing you should want most is God's Kingdom and doing what God wants. Then all these things you need will be given to you. So don't worry about tomorrow, because tomorrow will have its own worries. Each day has enough trouble of its own."

Matthew 22: verse 37; Jesus said, "Love the Lord your God with all your heart, all your soul, and all your mind."

In Matthew 12:23; and Mark 4:20; "Jesus said that those who hear the Word; understand it, receive, accept and welcome it. It will bear fruit –some yielding **30,** some **60,** and some **100**-fold!"

Mark 4: verses 24-25; "Everything that is hidden will be made clear and every secret thing will be made known. You people who can hear me listen! Think carefully about what you hear. The way you give to others is the way God will give to you, but God will give you even more. Those who have understanding will be given more. But those who do not have the understanding, even what they have will be taken away from them."

Matthew 19:29; and Mark 10:30; "Jesus said that those who have had to give up relationships or property for his sake would receive it all back multiplied by **100 times** in this lifetime and they would also inherit eternal life."

When God makes a promise, he obligates himself to keep it. When we do what is required of us, he does what he said he would. Obey God, and you obligate him to keep his word. You can obligate God through your obedience and to His Word and commandments. "I will open the windows of heaven for you, and pour out all the blessings you need." Say's the Lord.

Proverbs 10: verse 22; "The blessings of the Lord—it makes truly rich, and he adds no sorrow with it." (Neither does toiling increase it). When God blesses you, He really blesses you. You must realize it's not dependent on your work alone, but on your faith in God.

Deuteronomy 28: verses 1-14; "You must completely obey the Lord your God, and you must carefully follow all of his commands I am giving you today. Then the Lord your God will make you greater than any other nation on earth. Obey the Lord your God so that all these blessings will come and stay with you:

"You will be blessed in the city and blessed in the country. Your children will be blessed, as well as your crops; your herds will be blessed with calves and your flocks with lambs. Your baskets in your kitchens will be blessed. You will be blessed when you come in and blessed when you go out. The Lord will help defeat the enemies that come to fight you. They will attack you from one direction, but they will run from you in seven directions."

"The Lord your God will bless you with full barns, and He will bless everything you do. He will bless the land he is giving you. The Lord will make you his Holy people, as he promised. But you must obey His commands and do what He wants you to do. Then everyone on earth will see that you are the Lord's people, and they will be afraid of you. The Lord will make you rich: you will have many children, your animals will have many young, and your land will give good crops. It is the land the Lord promised your ancestors he would give to you."

"The Lord will open His heavenly storehouse so that the skies send rain on your land at the right time, and he will bless everything you do. You will lend to other nations (other believers), but you will not need to borrow from them. The Lord will make you like the head and not the tail. You will be on top and not the bottom. But you must obey the commands of the Lord your God that I am giving you today, being careful to keep them. Do not disobey anything I command you today. Do exactly as I command, and do not follow other gods or serve them."

John 15: verses 10-11; "I have obeyed my Father's commands, and I remain in his love. In the same way, if you obey my commands, you will remain in my love. I have told you these things so that you can have the same joy that I have and so that your joy will be the fullest possible joy."

2 Corinthians 9: verses 6-9; "Remember this:" "The person who plants a little will have a small harvest, but the person who plants a lot will have a big harvest. Each one should give as you have decided in your heart to give. You should not be sad when you give. God loves the person who gives happily. And God can give you more blessing than you need. Then you will always have plenty of everything-enough to give to every good work. It is written in the scriptures: He gives freely to the poor. The things he does are right and will continue forever."

Psalms 112: verse 9; "God is the one who gives seed to the farmer and bread for food. He will give you all the seed you need and make it grow so there will be a great harvest from your goodness. He will make you rich in every way so you can always give freely. And your giving to us will cause many to give thanks to God. It is proof of your faith. Many people will praise God because you **obey** the good News of Christ-The gospel you say you believe-and because you freely share with them and all others. And when they pray, they will wish they could be with you because of the great grace that God has given. Thanks be to God for his gift that is too wonderful for words!"

God, often times uses his people (believers) to bless others; at times he will tell them and you what to do, and we become blessings for each other through God by obeying Him. Yes, God can speak to you in an audible voice, which sounds just like he's right beside you, or it can be that still small voice that you feel and hear way deep down inside your spirit.

God spoke to me with an audible voice for the first time; one day when I had just pulled into my driveway from running errands, he said "Sell your watch", I said what? "I'm not going to sell my watch!" As I got out of my car and walked towards my front door, and looked around like... who was that? And it was then that I realized it was God. I was going through hard times, and I owned a Rolex Watch that was a precious sentimental gift given to me many years back, I didn't want to sell it, but I did. I had been praying and talking to God about my circumstances and He listened, just like His Word says. "I never mentioned my Rolex." God knows everything about you; when God asks you to do something, it is always linked to a blessing or a miracle; He has already got it set up for you. You just need to obey what He tells you to do and see how He will move on your behalf and see what He will do. *It will always be great!*

It's incredible when we know Jesus is with us in the midst of our daily, routine lives. In the middle of cleaning the house or driving somewhere...He stops us...in our tracks and makes His presence known. Often it is in the middle of the most mundane task that He lets us know, He is there with us. We realize, then, that there can be no "ordinary" moments for people who live their lives with Jesus.

Psalms 37: verse 5; "Commit everything you do to the Lord. Trust Him to help you do it, and He will."

If God is asking you to do something, get excited about it because that means he's already got it set up for you! You create a season of success every time you obey an instruction from God. And when God tells you to do something don't wait, because there is an anointing on it, do it right away! And where God leads, he will provide for you all the way.

In the Bible, when God says He is committed to you. He means committed no matter what; He wants you to commit everything you do to Him, so He can help you succeed. His goal is to enhance your life not limit it!

Because of God's excessive blessings, obedience becomes fun and very rewarding now and in heaven!

Deuteronomy 7: verse 9; "So know that the Lord your God is God, the faithful God. He will keep His agreement of love for a thousand lifetimes for people who love Him and obey His commands."

10

~~~

FORGIVENESS
AND RESTORATION

If you've made some mistakes in your life, and we all have, remember God's not looking for perfect people; He's looking for those whose hearts are turned towards Him. Let His love draw you and renew you! God makes all things new!

The key to successful relationships is love, forgiveness, and never holding grudges or taking offense; and having mercy, grace and kindness...in a way that can only come through knowing God intimately.

Maybe you're face to face with someone who doesn't deserve to be forgiven. Through Jesus' grace, you can forgive. Only when you are bathed in God's forgiveness can you extend that same, rich, ungrudging forgiveness to others.

Matthew 6: verses 14-15; "Yes, if you forgive others for their sins, your Father in heaven will also forgive you for your sins. But if you don't forgive others, your Father in heaven will not forgive your sins."

Matthew 18: verses 21-22; "Lord, when my fellow believer sins against me, how many times must I forgive him? Should I forgive him as many as seven times? Jesus answered, "I tell you, you must forgive him more than seven times. You must forgive him even if he wrongs you seventy times seven."

Mark 11: verse 25; "When you are praying, if you are angry with someone forgive him so that your Father in heaven will also forgive your sins."

Colossians 2: verse 3:13; "Get along with each other, and forgive each other. If someone does wrong to you, forgive that person because the Lord forgave you."

Proverbs 16: verse 6; "Love and truth bring forgiveness of sin. By respecting the Lord you will avoid evil."

Proverbs 18: verse 14; "The will to live can get through sickness, but no one can live with a broken spirit."

Luke 6: verse 37; "Don't judge other people, and you will not be judged. Don't accuse others of being guilty, and you will not be accused of being guilty. Forgive and you will be forgiven."

Hebrews 8: verse 12; "I will forgive them for the wicked things they did, and I will not remember their sins anymore."

2 Corinthians 2: verses 5-11; "Someone there among you has caused sadness; he caused sadness to all in some way. The punishment that most of you gave him was enough for him. But now you should forgive him and comfort him to keep him from having too much sadness and giving up completely. So I beg you to show that you love him. I wrote you to test you and to see if you obey in everything. If you forgive someone, I also forgive him. And what I have forgiven if I had anything to forgive-I forgave it for you as Christ were with me. I did this so that Satan would not win anything from us, because we know very well what Satan's plans are."

We all find forgiveness exceedingly difficult. Sometimes forgiveness comes so hard that we can release our grudges only one level at a time. This means forgiveness is often granted only at superficial levels. These are *qualified* forgiveness. A key word is *if*. "I'll forgive you, *if* you show proper remorse..."

Another key word is *when*. "I'll forgive you *when* I am able. You've got to give me some time to work through this..."

A second level is *partial* forgiveness. The key word here is *but*. "I'll forgive you, *but*...please get out of my life..." You must do forgiveness.

We *do* our way into better feelings. We do not feel our way into better doing. If we wait until all that bitterness is swept out of the corners of our feelings before we do right by someone who has hurt us, we might just as well give up. The bad feelings may never completely go away. But if you begin now dealing with that person, as if he had been totally forgiven and as if all the bad feelings were gone, giving him full person-hood and affirmation, somehow the bitterness eventually dissipates. **Jesus** didn't just *tell* us how to forgive, he *showed* us how on the cross. (From *Finding the Heart to Go On* by Lynn Anderson)

Romans 13: verse 2; "Do not change yourselves to be like the people of this world, but be changed within by a new way of thinking. Then you will be able to decide what God wants for you; you will know what is good and pleasing to him and what is perfect.

Jeremiah 29: verse 11; "Promises that God has great plans in store for you, and when you choose to follow His leading, He will guide you to a path of victory in every area of your life! You are born to win!"

One of the main keys to overcoming disappointments in life is learning to let go of the past. You let go of the past by choosing to forgive those who have hurt or wronged you by believing that God will restore to you anything that was taken. When you receive Christ forgiveness in your own life, you are released from the pressure to make up for the past mistakes or failures. You begin to experience the bright future God has in store for you.

No matter what has happened in the past, God is a God of restoration, and He will restore what the enemy has stolen from you.

Lamentations 5: verse 21; "Bring us back to you, Lord, and we will return. Make our days as they were before."

Don't keep secrets, confess it and get rid of it and let it go; so it doesn't kill you and steal your blessings. Call it what it is, and ask Jesus to forgive you, and he will forgive you. But don't be tempted to do it again.

1 John 3: verse 21; "says that a guilty conscience hinders communication with our heavenly Father."

That's why it's so important to stay true to your conscience and quickly repent if you've made a mistake.

Accept God's mercy and forgiveness today, and look forward to the wonderful plans He has for your future.

God promises to restore double to those who have hope in Him. When God restores something, He doesn't just set things back to the way they were before, He goes above and beyond. He makes things better than they were before! God can restore you and bring you twice as strong, twice as favored, twice as influential and twice as blessed on the other side! That's a reason to have hope today. And that's a reason to rejoice!

God has the power and the ability to restore broken families. He can restore lost dreams and work miracles beyond what you could ever imagine in the natural!

Choose to believe and look for His goodness and know that with God, all things are possible and everlasting joy will be yours!

11

WHO GOES TO HELL?

Revelation 21: verse 8; Describes who goes to hell: "the cowardly, the unbelieving, the vile, the murderers, the sexually immoral, those who practice magic arts, the idolaters and **all liars**–their place will be in the fiery lake of burning sulfur. A critically important word in this list is **"the unbelieving."** Who are the unbelievers that go to hell?

John 3: verse 18; "Is clear that those who do not believe in Jesus Christ, suffer eternal punishment, "whoever does not believe stands condemned already because they have not believed in the name of God's one and only Son."

1 Corinthians 6: verses 9-11; "Surely you know that people who do wrong will not inherit God's kingdom. Do not be fooled. Those who sin sexually, worship idols, take part in adultery, those who are male prostitutes, or men who have other sexual relations with other men, those who steal, are greedy, get drunk, lie about others, or rob... these people will not inherit God's kingdom. In the past some of you were like that, but you were washed clean. You were made holy, and you were made right with God in the name of the Lord Jesus Christ and in the Spirit of God."

Psalm 1: verses 1-6; "Happy are those who don't listen to the wicked, who don't go where sinners go, who don't do what evil people do. They love the Lord's teachings, and they think about those teachings day and night. They are strong like a tree planted by a river. The tree produces fruit in season, and its leaves don't die. Everything they do will succeed." "But the wicked people are not like that. They are like chaff that the wind blows away. So the wicked will not escape God's punishment. Sinners will not worship with God's people. This is because the LORD takes care of his people, but the wicked will be destroyed."

Matthew 13: verse 41; "The angels will throw them into the blazing furnace, where the people will cry and grind their teeth with pain."

Matthew 22: verse 13; "According to Jesus, hell knows only one sound, the "weeping and gnashing of teeth."

12

~~~

MAKE TIME FOR JESUS

We all spend time with the things we love the most, and a relationship with Jesus is very personal and intimate. Intimacy does not happen overnight, it requires time, mutual trust, heart to heart, soul to soul, spirit to spirit, integrity, commitment and listening. Jesus desires intimacy with you more than you do. I have made it a priority to get to know God and Jesus personally; being faithful, obedient, and willing, meditating on God's Word and including Him in everything I do and need; the fruit of that is the anointing of the precious life changing fellowship of the Holy Spirit, and God's divine favor and grace that is visible in my life. God revealed himself strong to me and my twin sisters during one of the darkest times in our lives, we had a Supernatural Encounter with God, a "Biblically Prophetic Event in the Sky" that I also prophesied about fourteen days before it happened! I am so in love with our heavenly Father God and our Lord Jesus Christ, He is divinely supreme, and He is the greatest love I have ever known! The love I feel from him within my soul and spirit; is the kind of love I have been yearning for all of my life.

Ephesians 3: verses 18-21; "And I pray that you and all God's holy people will have the power to understand the greatness of Christ's love...how wide and how long and how high and how deep that love is. Christ's love is greater than anyone can ever know, but I pray that you will be able to know that love. Then you can be filled with the fullness of God. **With God's power working in us, God can do much, much more than anything we can ask or imagine.** To Him be the glory in the church and in Christ Jesus for all time, forever and ever. Amen."

Although God's love for us cannot be measured by any comprehensible standards, God wants us to know this ocean of love. The promises of God's love and forgiveness are as real, as sure, as positive as human words can make them. But like describing the ocean, its total beauty cannot be understood until it is actually seen. It is the same with God's love. Until you actually accept it, until you actually experience it, until you actually possess true peace with God, no one can describe its wonders to you.

It is not something that you can do with your mind. Your finite mind is not capable of dealing with anything as great as the love of God. Your mind might have difficulty explaining how a black cow can eat green grass and give white milk...but you drink the milk and are nourished by it. Your mind can't reason through all the intricate processes that take place when you plant a small flat seed that produces a huge vine bearing luscious red and green watermelons...but you eat them and enjoy them! You can't understand radio but you listen. Your mind can't explain the electricity that may be creating the light by which you are reading at this very moment...but you know that it's there and that it is making it possible for you to read! (From *Peace with God* by Billy Graham)

When you want what you've never had, you need to do what you've never done. Start your relationship with God, right where you are right now... this very minute! Nothing is impossible, to those who believe in a God that never fails!

Psalm 37: verse 4; "Delight yourself also in the LORD, and He shall give you the desires of your heart."

Psalm 116 verses 1-2; "I love the Lord, because he listens to my prayers for help. He paid attention to me, so I will call to Him for help as long as I live."

Start your relationship with Jesus right where you are! It's about a transformation; learn to yield to the Spirit of God. He wants you to submit your heart to Him. Jesus love's, love; and He loves worship and sacrifice. Worship creates a Supernatural element around you, and that's when Jesus will show up by His Spirit and you can feel His presence, then your faith begins to increase. When I began my personal relationship with God it was right here in my home. In the beginning when I attended church services on line, and I still do, I would always skip the worship part; then one morning the Holy Spirit said;

"Father wishes to see you worship," and that got my attention! From that moment on, I began to worship. I learned the power of worship, when we are in need of a breakthrough or an answer about direction and times of refreshing, it will often come to us in worship. Download your favorite worship songs or purchase some and get into some good worship, it will always lift you up when you exalt the Lord. I was never one who liked to read, so I began reading the Bible each night when I went to bed so I would have no distractions, reading The Word aloud softly to activate God's power is how you meditate on God's Word, not by sitting and saying nothing! It is by faith that we speak God's Word out of our mouths to activate His power, so whatever it is you are praying for will manifest and come to pass! Your miracle is in your mouth!

Psalm 46: verse 10; God says, "Be quiet and know that I am God. I will be supreme over all nations; I will be supreme in the earth."

Making time to get alone with God may seem tough– at times even impossible. In our world today, most people are used to having constant activity: computers, cell phones, television, email and video games. Stress, deadlines, relationships and responsibilities compete for your time; but the Bible tells us that we need to stop and be still so we can focus on God. Especially during difficult times or when you are facing a challenge!

Remember, our battles are spiritual battles. The people in your life aren't the source of your problems, the forces of darkness are. When you choose to be still and know that the Greater One lives on the inside of you, you are putting yourself in a position of strength. We have to learn to fight like God would fight. You don't return evil for evil. You don't return anger for anger. But when somebody does you wrong, you go out and help someone else. Now, this is really a spiritual secret and a lot of people never get it. If you can learn how to fight like this, you will win every battle.

In the midst of your daily storms, make it a point to be still and set your mind on Him. God's Word is "need specific." Look up the scriptures in the Bible that apply to the things you need in your life and meditate on those words out loud, that's when you will see your miracles come. Biblical Scriptures were created by God to help us! **Let God be God; Seek Him** and let him bathe you in his glory so that both your breath and your troubles are sucked from your very soul. Be still. Talk to God, and make your words meaningful and personal. Be open and willing. He wants to move in your life; He only comes where He is wanted. Delight yourself in the Lord; He loves it when we do that. And over a period of time as you do this, it will become so natural to you that it's simply effortless; you won't want to go without it.

Being IN LOVE with GOD allows you to move from duty to DEVOTION! You don't HAVE TO follow his commands...you WANT TO because you are IN LOVE WITH JESUS! WITH ALL YOUR HEART!

Mark 4: verses 26-34; Jesus Uses a Story about Seed. Jesus said. "The Kingdom of God is like someone who plants seed in the ground. Night and day, whether the person is asleep or awake, the seed still grows, but the person does not know how it grows, by itself the earth produces grain. First the plant grows, then the head, and then all the grain in the head. When the grain is ready, the farmer cuts it, because this is the harvest time."

Then Jesus said, "How can I show you what the Kingdom of God is like? What story can I use to explain it? The Kingdom of God is like a mustard seed, the smallest seed you plant in the ground. But when planted this seed grows and becomes the largest of all garden plants. It produces large branches, and the wild birds can make nests in its shade." Jesus used many stories like these to teach the crowd God's message, as much as they could understand.

Luke 17: verse 6; "The Lord said, "If your faith were the size of a mustard seed, you could say to this mulberry tree, 'Dig yourself up and plant yourself in the sea,' and it would obey you."

Philippians 4: verses 4-7; "Be full of joy in the Lord always. I will say it again, be full of joy. Let everyone see that you are gentle and kind. The Lord is coming soon. Do not worry about anything, but pray and ask God for everything you need, always giving thanks. And God's peace, which is so great we cannot understand it, will keep your hearts and minds in Christ Jesus."

The Lords joy is unspeakable and full of glory! When you are sensitive to the Spirit and in that secret place of the presence of God, *pressing in (meditating)* and praying and worshiping, you begin to fill his joy bubble up inside your belly; at times you will be beside yourself with laughter that will go on and on, even when nothing in your life is funny at all. This is also when miracles will happen. The "Joy of the Lord" is where you will get your strength. Jesus Christ, the Son of God, longs to share in and to be the source of the laughter and the joy we all too rarely know. When you get a touch from God, you will never be the same!

When GOD touches you, you will endeavor to try and tell others about it your whole life...because it's hard to put into words; when you are saturated into the realms of His glory; it's like nothing you have ever felt or known before. And His touch will elevate you to a whole new level! One touch from God can keep you going for a very long time. I mean, just one little, special touch from God can just strengthen you and energize you in such an amazing way!

Romans 15: verses 2 & 15; "We who are strong in faith should help the weak with their weaknesses, and not please only ourselves. Let each of us please our neighbors for their good, to help them be stronger in faith. I pray the God who gives hope will fill you with much joy and peace while you trust in Him. Then your hope will overflow by the power of the Holy Spirit."

Hebrews 11: verse 1-2; what is Faith? "Faith comes by the Spirit of God, faith has to do with your heart and your spirit; faith means being sure of the things we hope for and knowing that something is real even if we do not see it."

We should always have child-like faith. Faith purifies the heart and gives us security, confidence and excessive blessings. When we do things in faith; it is faith filled God inspired action that allows our miracles to come. "Calling what is not in our lives to be what it should be."

Everything you're ever going to get from God comes by faith. Faith believes in the integrity of the one who promises. If God promised it, He is able to perform it! The area we need to work on more than anything else is patients. The promises He has said will come to pass because God does not lie. "Faith calls it done, without any other proof in the natural; says the Lord." Faith is now; Faith never talks of anything but the promise of God. You only need a mustard size seed of faith. It's time to release your faith to God in prayer, and activate your faith. "Faith without works is nothing!"

13

～～

PEOPLE KNOW YOU
BY YOUR WORDS

Matthew 12: verses 33-37; "If you want good fruit, you must make the tree good. If your tree is not good, it will have bad fruit. A tree is known by the kind of fruit it produces. You snakes! You are evil people, so how can you say anything good? The mouth speaks the things that are in the heart. Good people have good things in their hearts, and so they say good things. But evil people have evil in their hearts, so they say evil things. And I tell you that on Judgment Day people will be responsible for every careless thing they have said. The words you have said will be used to judge you. Some of your words will prove you right, but some of your words will prove you guilty."

Luke 6: verses 43-45; "A good tree does not produce bad fruit, nor does a bad tree produce good fruit. Each tree is known by its own fruit. People don't gather figs from thorn bushes, and they don't get grapes from bushes. Good people bring good things out of the good they stored in their hearts. But evil people bring evil things out of the evil they stored in their hearts. People speak the things that are in their hearts."

You are a seed; your mother and father were the ones who planted the seed to conceive you. Everything in existence today comes from a seed. Your success and your destiny are determined by you because you are a seed. Inside of us is everything we will ever need. In other words, choose to protect and have self-control: Your thoughts are seeds, your attitude it is a seed, your words are seeds and your actions are all seeds.

Every word you speak is a seed for your future. And all of these determine your success and your destiny. Seeds that you sow determine how far you will go. Don't be your biggest hindrance in your future and don't break people down with your words. Every part of your life will be affected, and also children will follow your example and become generations of good or bad seeds. Move with the wisdom and guidance of God in every area of your life. And you need to be in agreement with everyone you associate with about your faith.

Proverbs 18: verse 21; "What you say can mean life or death. Those who speak with care will be rewarded."

Remember the power of the tongue, (whatever comes out of your mouth), can **literally** be the difference between **life** and **death.** Words are containers of either creative power or destructive power. **Every word is like a seed,** and can bring good or bad into your life. So be very careful with the things that you say always. Don't grieve the Holy Spirit by the things that you say or by your actions. A mature and spiritually faithful person chooses words carefully, bringing good to change things, and is aware of how what you say effects people, what comes out of your mouth should grace people. Do not say harmful things; say what people need to become stronger.

James 3: verses 13-17; True Wisdom, Are there those among you who are truly wise and understanding? Then they should show it by living right and doing good things with gentleness that comes from wisdom. But if you are selfish and have bitter jealousy in your hearts, do not brag. Your bragging is a lie that hides the truth. That kind of "wisdom" does not come from God but from the world. It is not spiritual; it is from the devil. Where jealousy and selfishness are, there will be confusion and every kind of evil. **But the wisdom that comes from God is first of all pure, then peaceful, gentle, and easy to please.** This wisdom is always ready to help those who are troubled and to do good for others. It is always fair and honest.

Proverbs 10: verses 11, 20 & 21; "The words of a good person give life, like a fountain of water, but the words of the wicked contain nothing but violence." "The words of a good person are like pure silver, but an evil person's thoughts are worth very little." "Good people's words will help many others, but fools will die because they don't have wisdom."

The Spirit and Human Nature; **Galatians 5: verses 16-26;** "So I tell you; live by following the Spirit. Then you will not do what your sinful selves want. Our sinful selves want what is against the Spirit, and the Spirit wants what is against our sinful selves. The two are against each other, so you cannot do just what you please. The wrong things the sinful self does are: being sexually unfaithful, not being pure, taking part in sexual sins, worshiping gods, doing witchcraft, hating, making trouble, being jealous, being angry, being selfish, making people angry with each other, causing division among people, feeling envy, being drunk, having wild and wasteful parties, and doing other things like these will no inherit God's kingdom. **But the Spirit produces the fruit of love, joy, peace, patience, kindness, goodness, faithfulness, gentleness and self-control.** Those who belong to Christ Jesus have crucified their own sinful selves. They have given up their old selfish feelings and the evil things they wanted to do. We get our new life from the Spirit, so we should follow the Spirit. We must not be proud or make trouble with each other or be jealous of each other."

James 3: verses 3-7; "When we put bits into the mouths of horses to make them obey us, we can control their whole bodies. Also a ship is very big, and it is pushed by strong winds. But a very little rudder controls that big ship, making it go wherever the pilot wants. It is the same with the tongue. It is a small part of the body, but it brags about great things. A big forest fire can be started with only a little flame. And the tongue is like a fire. It is a whole world of evil among the parts of our bodies. The tongue spreads its evil through the whole body. The tongue is set on fire by hell, and it starts a fire that influences all of life. It is wild and evil and full of deadly poison."

Luke 12: verses 2-3; "Everything that is hidden will be shown, and everything that is secret will be made known. What you have said in the dark will be heard in the light, and what you have whispered in an inner room will be shouted out from the roof tops."

Ephesians 4: verses 29-32; "When you talk, do not say harmful things, but say what people need...words that will help others become stronger. Then what you say will do good to those who listen to you. And do not make the Holy Spirit sad. The Spirit is God's proof that you belong to him. God gave you the Spirit to show that God will make you free when the final day comes. Do not be bitter and angry or mad. Never shout angrily or say things to hurt others. Never do anything evil. Be kind and loving to each other, and forgive each other just as God forgave you in Christ."

Psalm 139: verses 1-5; "Lord, you have examined me and know all about me. You know when I sit down and when I get up. You know my thoughts before I think them. You know where I go and where I lie down. You know thoroughly everything I do. Lord, even before I say a word, you already know it. You are all around me... in front and in back...and have put your hand on me.

Your knowledge is amazing to me; it is more than I can understand."

Colossians 3: verses 15-17; "Let the peace that Christ gives control your thinking, because you were all called together in one body" to have peace. Always be thankful. Let the teaching of Christ live in you richly." "Use all wisdom to teach and instruct each other by singing psalms, hymns, and spiritual songs with thankfulness in your hearts to God. Everything you do or say should be done to obey Jesus your Lord. And in all you do, give thanks to God the Father through Jesus."

God is sovereign over angels, principalities and powers, demon spirits and Satan himself. He rules in heaven, on earth and under the earth.

God is; all knowing, all seeing, all present and all powerful! God see's everything! Jesus is the unseen guest in your house and He is with you everywhere you go!

Begin your miracle journey with your words. God has given us the instruction manual for a victorious life in His Word!

14

~~

THE POWER OF
PRAYER AND PRAISE

Prayer gives us immediate access to the Creator of the Universe, "God the Father!" The very moment a need arises in your life of any kind, the first thing you should do is pray to God, in the name of Jesus. There is power in prayer, and this is the only way miracles will happen! God wants you to depend on Him, no matter what your need is. And when you pray, He listens attentively. When we are hurting, so many times we look to other people to help us feel better only to discover they don't have everything we need.

James 5: verses 15-16; "And the prayer that is said with faith will make the sick person well; the Lord will heal that person. And if the person has sinned, the sins will be forgiven. Confess your sins to each other and pray for each other so God can heal you. When a believing person prays, great things happen!"

Ephesians 6: verses 10-12; "Finally, be strong in the Lord and his great power. Put on the full armor of God so that you can fight against the devil's evil tricks. Our fight is not against people on earth but against the rulers and authorities and the powers of this world's darkness, against the spiritual powers of evil in the heavenly world."

Ephesians 6: verses 16-18; "And also use the shield of faith with which you can stop all the burning arrows of the Evil One. Accept God's salvation as your helmet, and take the sword of the Spirit, which is the word of God. **Pray in the Spirit at all times with all kinds of prayers, asking for everything you need.**"

1 John 5: verses 14-15; "And this is the boldness we have in God's presence: that if we ask God for anything that agrees with what he wants, he hears us. If we know he hears us every time we ask him, we know we have what we ask from him."

John 14: verses 12-14; "I tell you the truth, whoever believes in me will do the same things I do. Those who believe will do even greater things than these, because I am going to be with the Father." "And if you ask for anything in my name, I will do it for you so that the Father's glory will be shown through the Son. If you ask me for anything in my name, I will do it."

John 16: verse 24; "Until now you have not ask for anything in my name. Ask and you will receive, so that your joy will be the fullest possible joy."

God desires you to pray so specifically that when you get the answer, you will know that only he could have sent it.

I think maybe the problem for some people is they are thinking to small when it comes to their prayer life. You need to be aggressive and ask God size prayers. When we pray in faith according to God's will, we see the greatness of His power demonstrated in our lives! God wants us to be bold when we pray!

Mark 11: verse 24; "So I tell you to believe that you have received the things ask for in prayer, and God will give them to you."

Every day there should be something we are praying about, something we're asking for that seems impossible, and something that we cannot achieve on our own. This kind of faith will propel you to new heights and help you to live a whole new level of fulfillment. Ask, believe and receive; and remember to enjoy the journey!

Matthew 18: verses 19-20; "If two or more agree on earth about something; and pray for it in Jesus name it shall be done!" This is true because if two or three people come together in my name, I am there with them."

James 4: verses 2-8; "You want things, but you don' have them. So you are ready to kill and are jealous of other people, but you still cannot get what you want. So you argue and fight. **You do not get what you want because you don't ask God**. Or when you ask, you don't receive it because it's for the reason you ask is wrong. You want things so you can use them for your own pleasure "So give yourselves completely to God. Stand against the devil, and the devil will run from you. Come near to God, and God will come near to you".

If you have prayed for something and your prayer has not been answered; it's most likely because you have a hidden secret that you need to stop doing and ask Jesus to forgive you for and close doors in your life that need to be closed. And be patient; God always wants to teach us a lesson just the same as our earthly father would, because he loves you and wants the best for you. He is on your side.

Good things take time before there good...develop an attitude of trust. God can change situations. His name is Deliverer... One of the most often repeated commands in the Bible is to "wait on the Lord." Waiting on him grows you up", it keeps your eyes off yourself and on Him; and it gives you staying power.

Mark 11: verses 22-24; "Jesus said, "Have faith in God. I tell you the truth, you can say to this mountain, 'Go, fall into the sea.' And if you have no doubts in your mind and believe that what you say will happen God will do it for you. So I tell you to believe that you have received the things you have ask for in prayer, and God will give them to you."

Galatians 6: verses 1-10; "Brothers and sisters, if someone in your group does something wrong, you who are spiritual should go to that person and gently help make him right again. But be careful, because you might be tempted to sin, too. By helping each other with your troubles, you truly obey the law of Christ. If anyone thinks he is important when he really is not, he is only fooling himself. Each person should judge his own actions and not compare himself with others. Then he can be proud of what he himself has done. Each person must be responsible for himself. Anyone who is learning the teaching of God should share all the good things he has with his teacher."

2 Corinthians 1: verses 3-4; "Praise be to God and Father of our Lord Jesus Christ. God is the Father who is full mercy and of all comfort." "He comforts us every time we have trouble, so when others have trouble, we can comfort them with the same comfort God gives us."

The Holy Spirit, who dwells on the inside of us, knows us better than anyone else, and when life is painful, He has the ability to bring strength and healing right where we hurt. Yes, the Lord often uses others to bring us comfort, but running to God first opens the door for Him to help us in the best way possible.

Psalm 9: verses 1-2; "I will praise you, Lord, with all my heart. **I will tell all the miracles you have done.** I will be happy because of you; God Most High, I will sing praises to your name."

Remember the power of praise. **Praise creates a supernatural element, an atmosphere for miracles**! Jesus is the focus, the reason, and the joy of our worship. Humble yourself to worship the Lord Jesus Christ with songs, to love and magnify His Holy name because it is the highest form of prayer. When the praises go up, the blessings come down!

Friends, I want you to know that God has you covered. I think many of us have a mindset that says, oh, I don't want to bother the Lord with that. But the truth is: the One who knows you the best is the One who desires to help you the most. And He is with you_everywhere you go.

Matthew 7: verses 7 -8; ASK GOD FOR WHAT YOU NEED! "Ask, and God will give it to you. Search and you will find. Knock and the door will open for you. Yes, everyone who asks will receive. Everyone who searches will find. And everyone who knocks will have the door open.

Surround yourself with the right people and you can begin to fulfill the dreams God gives you. Put yourself in a relationship with people who are not only like-minded, but are also seeking to honor God in their own lives. If your friends don't point you towards God's goal for you, then they're not very good friends. You want to be around dream-builder's not dream-crashers.

For all the single ladies and gentleman of every age out there; looking for true love, ASK GOD! A man or woman of God, who knows how to exercise the authority and power that God has given him in his everyday life is very appealing; this time around, I'm letting God lead me to my soul-mate. When you want what you've never had, you need to do what you've never done. I don't go anywhere or do anything without involving God! Are you getting this yet? When we interact with God, as we should be, in everything we do and desire, we will ALWAYS WIN! At long last you will be on your way to fulfilling your destiny in every area of your life; what He has planned for us is far greater than anything you or I could have ever imagined. When you get a revelation of this, it will literally change your life!

Be excited about who you are in Christ. When you're passionate about whom you are; it brings honor to God. That's when God will breathe in your direction and the seeds of greatness in you will take root and begin to flourish.

15

~

THE FULL GOSPEL
OF JESUS CHRIST
& REPENTANCE

What makes the Bible unique is that it doesn't just commemorate the past...it provides guidance for today and for hope for tomorrow. You can find your name and face in its pages. It's a living, dynamic, hopeful expectation of God's plans for the future. (By Max Lucado)

2 Timothy 3: verses 16-17; "All Scripture is given by God and is useful for teaching, for showing people what is wrong in their lives, for correcting faults, and for teaching how to live right. Using the Scriptures, the person who serves God will be capable, having all that is needed to do every good work."

Ephesians 1: verses 13-14; "So it is with you. When you heard the true teaching...the Good News about your salvation...you believed in Christ. And in Christ, God put his special mark of ownership on you by giving you the Holy Spirit that he had promised. That Holy Spirit is the guarantee that we will receive what God has promised for his people until God gives full freedom to those who are his...to bring praise to God's glory."

Romans 15: verses 4-6; "Everything that was written in the past was written to teach us. The Scriptures gives us patience and encouragement so we have hope. Patience and encouragement come from God. And I pray that God will help you all agree with each other the way Christ Jesus wants. Then you will all be joined together, and you will give glory to God the Father of our Lord Jesus Christ."

Psalms 19: verse 18; "Open my eyes to see the miracles in your teachings."

I felt I should get out and find myself a home church and be around other believers and share my testimonies and hear theirs. And well, that was a lot harder than I ever expected. I had no idea that so many churches were so political and religious; I quickly learned that word "Religion" was not a good spirit. Religion is always looking for what is wrong, instead of what is right. It's the spirit of religion that denies the power of God. It is through God's people that He displays His Glory, not through religion! God doesn't call us to be religious; He calls us to be a light shining in a dark world! It's about the Gospel "The Good News" of Jesus Christ, the Word of God! I went to four different churches in my area; only to find a sermon would last for thirty minutes, not really helping anybody and two out of four of those churches never once spoke of the Holy Spirit; and if they did, it was in secret.

There was no one I could talk to in those specific churches about the "Gifts of the Spirit" and the wonderful things God was doing in my life. Even the most beautiful churches with all the bells and whistles, were the churches that I felt the most empty when I left. Because they weren't helping anybody, they were not speaking the whole truth about the Word of God. You were the same when you walked out, as you were when you walked in; never feeling the pure authentic presence of God there that I felt in my own home.

Unfortunately, there are so many churches in the world today that are being run like a business franchise. And they are not really helping the people who come to them to learn about the whole truth of God's Word; leaving some of the most important parts of the Word of God out, like the anointing of the "Holy Spirit" and your, "Tithe" which is your giving to honor God. I am really amazed how many places do not teach on Tithe and the anointing of the Holy Spirit, it saddens me. How can anyone who does not know about Tithing receive supernatural financial provision from God? How can anyone who doe's not know about the anointing of the Holy Spirit speak in tongues or receive the gift of prophecy? How can the people of those churches receive all that God has for them, when the pastors of those churches have not?

Please, find a "Spirit filled Church" that teaches the full Gospel of Jesus Christ including the Holy Spirit, so you can have all that God has for you! Where you can feel the pure authentic presence of God, and actually be part of a miracle yourself if needed, and see miracles take place with your own eyes, with people getting healed of sickness and diseases and being saved and set free from religion and every other stronghold on their lives.

Some people think that just because they are a good person and they go to a church once in a while, that they will be blessed in every way and have eternal life in heaven. And that is just not true. **You must be saved, (born again)**! I personally have been around adults who have said; "I'm a good person or I was baptized when I was a little boy or a little girl, I don't need to be baptized or saved again." Meanwhile they have certainly sinned at some point in their adult life. (We have all sinned, at some point in our lives we have tried to live on our own, apart from God.) And they have all hell coming against them in their personal life, their families, relationships, their marriages, their children's life's and their finances. And wonder why?

Obadiah: Verse 3-4; "Your pride has fooled you, you who live in the hollow places of the cliff, Your home is up high, you who say to yourself, 'No one can bring me down to the ground.' Even if you fly high like an eagle and make your nest among the stars, I will bring you down from there," says the Lord."

If your experiencing spiritual dissatisfaction and you don't have a hunger for God, and you have exhausted all of your resources and your still in the same place, it's because of disobedience and sin and unbelief; it will harden your heart little by little and you will feel stagnate. You have to yield yourself and submit to God with all of your heart in order to receive access to God's Supernatural Power. The condition of your heart is the condition of your life. Hard heartedness blocks miracles and blessings from God. If you have un-forgiveness, bitterness, jealousy and pride, these are also sin. Repent of your sin and re-dedicate your life to Jesus today, so you can experience an intimate and very personal relationship with God. He looks at the heart and the mouth speaks what's in the heart.

If this is you, don't be stubborn or deceived; Deception is the enemy's greatest weapon, and it's the Spirit of Pride that will steal every miracle you and your family may need! Unless you are sure without a shadow of a doubt that you have never sinned, since you were baptized as a child, you need to be "Saved!" God's goodness is intended to lead you to repentance.

Romans 2: verses 4-5; "He has been very kind and patient, waiting for you to change, but you think nothing of his kindness. Perhaps you do not understand that God is kind to you so you will change your hearts and lives. But you are stubborn and refuse to change, so you are making your own punishment even greater on the day he shows his anger. On that day everyone will see God's right judgments.

God loves you so much and he has a perfect plan for every person; if you don't know God intimately, you have already missed the first step. God is responsible for the results, if you're not seeing results with God's favor and bearing good fruit in your everyday life and others cannot see the Fruit of the Spirit in your life, this is for you!

Proverbs 10: verse 17; "Whoever accepts correction is on the way to life, but whoever ignores correction will lead others away from life."

Psalm 86: verse 11; "On earth people will be loyal to God, and God's goodness will shine down from heaven."

Jeremiah 16: verses 7-8; "But the person who trusts in the LORD will be blessed. The Lord will show him that he can be trusted. He will be strong, like a tree planted near water that sends its roots by the stream. It is not afraid when the days are hot; its leaves are always green. It does not worry when a year of no rain comes; it always produces fruit."

John 15: verses 1-2 & 4-5; "I am the true vine; my Father is the gardener. He cuts off every branch of mine that does not produce fruit. And he trims and cleans every branch that produces fruit so that it will produce even more fruit." "Remain in me, and I will remain in you. A branch cannot produce fruit alone but must remain in the vine. In the same way, you cannot produce fruit alone, but must remain in me." "I am the vine and you are the branches. If any remain in me and I remain in them, they produce much fruit. But without me they can do nothing."

You can't be connected to the "Vine" and not have fruit. There are things in your life that are keeping you from producing fruit, and you have got to get rid of Carnality. You have to submit your flesh to the Word of God and continue to have fellowship and communion with God; He will import in you the revelation of truth and the process will start to happen as you yield yourself to Him. Don't let the devil trap you in your mind and flesh. What is of the soul will fade away, and what is of the spirit is eternal, walk by your faith not by your feelings. And the life of the Spirit has nothing to do with religion.

The fruit comes from your union with Christ, it is impossible without repentance to be fruitful. God has come to give us life and life more abundantly! And God cannot use you beyond the level of criticism you can handle, if there is none, than you're not doing anything and you're not a threat to the devil.

Psalm 51: verses 10-12; "Create in me a pure heart, God, and make my spirit right again. Do not send me away from you or take your Holy Spirit away from me. Give me back the joy of your salvation. Keep me strong by giving me a willing spirit."

Proverbs 15: verse 33; "Respect for the Lord will teach you wisdom. If you want to be honored, you must be humble. People may make plans in their minds, but only the Lord can make them come true."

It is better to humble yourself and be baptized and rededicate yourself many times throughout your life if needed, just to make sure you are right with God, than to have never done it all! So if this is you, please make your heart and your soul pure again, and say the Salvation Prayer included in my book; ask Jesus to come into your heart by doing it now and follow it up with a "Water Baptism" as soon as possible! Seek Him with all of your heart and your mind and your soul, and watch what happens in your life. I promise you will be transformed by the power of God; and the people who know you and love you will see your heart changed, and you will see the greatness of God's miracles and excessive blessings visible in your life too. God is waiting for you...and Jesus is waiting too. God wants to touch you and love on you! Keep honoring God; keep treating people right and the Lord will take you places you never thought you would be!

James 1: verses 26; "People who think they are religious but say things they should not say are just fooling themselves. Their "religion" is worth nothing."

James 4: verses 7-10; "So give yourselves completely to God. Stand against the devil, and the devil will run from you. Come near to God, and God will come near to you. You sinners, clean sin out of your lives. You, who are trying to follow God and the world at the same time, make your thinking pure. Be sad, cry and weep! Change your laughter into crying and your joy into sadness. Don't be too proud in the Lord's presence, and He will make you great."

1 John 2: verses 5-10; "God is light, and in Him there is no darkness at all." "So if we say we have

fellowship with God, but we continue living in darkness, we are liars and do not follow the truth. But if we live in the light, as God is in the light, we can share fellowship with each other. Then the blood of Jesus, God's Son, cleanses us from every sin. If we say we have no sin, we are fooling ourselves, and the truth is not in us. But if we are baptized he will forgive us our sins, because we can trust God to do what is right. He will cleanse us from all the wrongs we have done. If we say we have not sinned, we make God a liar, and we do not accept God's teaching."

Matthew 7: verses 21-23; "Not all those who say that I am their Lord will enter the kingdom of heaven. The only people who will enter the kingdom of heaven are those who do what my Father in heaven wants. On the last day many people will say to me, 'Lord, Lord, we spoke for you, and through you we forced out demons and did many miracles.' Then I will tell them clearly, 'Get away from me, you who do evil. I never knew you.'

1 John 2: verses 3-6; "We can be sure that we know God if we obey his commands. Anyone who says, "I know God," but does not obey God's commands is a liar, and the truth is not in that person. But if someone obeys God's teaching, then in that person God's love has truly reached its goal. This is how we can be sure we are living in God: Whoever says that he lives in God must live as Jesus lived."

Your heart is the resting place of the Spirit; you can't change your heart outside of the presence of God.

Something has to change on the inside of you before it will change on the outside of you.

The only way into the blessings of God is repentance! If you want anything He has promised; you have to take the first step to be "Born Again" and be the fruitful person God wants you to be. His miracles and excessive blessings are visible!

16

~

GOD'S WORD IS TRUE

God's Word is true and is the most beautiful expression of love ever written. No earthly image can actually portrait God's love for us. With a love so devoted, so sacrificial, so extreme...nothing can ever interfere. Nothing can squelch or diminish that love. You cannot fall beyond the reach of His love. You can't lose it. You can't change it, win it, or control it. His love extends before and beyond time, and He loved you before you knew him. When you choose to accept His love, you begin the most amazing relationship of your life. (By Max Lucado)

1 John 4: verses 7-10; "Dear friends, we should love each other, because love comes from God. Everyone who loves has become God's child and knows God. Whoever does not love, does not know God, because **God is love**. This is how God showed his love to us: He sent his one

and only Son into the world so that we could have life through him. This is what real love is: It is not our love for God; it is God's love for us in sending his Son to be the way to take away our sins."

1 John 4: verses 13-18; "We know that we live in God and he lives in us, because he gave us his Spirit. We have seen and can testify that the Father sent his Son to be the Savior of the world. Whoever confesses that Jesus is the Son of God has God living inside, and that person lives in God. And so we know the love that God has for us, and we trust that love. **God is love.** Those who live in love live in God, and God lives in them. This is how love is made perfect in us: that we can be without fear on the day God judges us, because in this world we are like Him. **Where God's love is, there is no fear, because God's perfect love drives out fear."**

John 3: verses 16-17; "God loved the world so much that he gave his one and only Son so that whoever believes in him may not be lost, but have eternal life. God did not send his Son into the world to judge the world guilty, but to save the world through him."

Hebrews 4: verses 12-13; "God's Word is alive and working and is sharper than a double-edged sword. It cuts all the way into us, where the soul and spirit are joined, to the center of our joints and bones. And it judges the thought and feeling in our hearts. Nothing in all the world can be hidden from God. Everything is clear and lies open before him, and to him we must explain the way we have lived."

Hebrews in the Bible states; "GOD REWARDS those who DILIGINTLY SEEK HIM, which means this: If we answer the call to ACTIVELY FELLOWSHIP with GOD, then we will see the POWER and LIFE of the HOLY SPIRIT break out of OUR spirits and SPREAD LIKE A WILDFIRE, transforming every area of our lives!"

When God begins to pour out His love in your life, he doesn't just pour in a little dab. When God invades your life, he begins to pour and pour, and the blessings get better and richer and deeper.

Matthew 6: verse 21; "Your heart will be where your treasure is."

Matthew 7: verses 24-28; "Everyone who hears my words and obeys them is like a wise man who built his house on a rock. It rained hard, the floods came, and the winds blew and hit the house. But it did not fall, because it was built on rock. Everyone who hears my words and does not obey them is like a foolish man who built his house on sand. It rained hard, the floods came, and the winds blew and hit the house, and it fell with a big crash." When Jesus finished saying these things the people were amazed at his teaching.

The Bible offers answers to crucial questions. It is the treasure map that leads us to God's highest treasure, eternal life. Not only should we read the Bible prayerfully, we should read it carefully. *Search and you will find, is the pledge.* The Bible is not a newspaper to be skimmed but rather a mine to be quarried. (By Max Lucado)

Proverbs 2: verses 4-5; "Search for your answers like silver, and hunt for it like hidden treasure. Then you will understand respect for the Lord, and you will find that you know God.

Philippians 4: verse 19; "God shall supply all your needs."

While this is a wonderful scripture, you must obey God's Word and give Him something to work with. This is why I have applied Biblical Scripture here in my book, to teach you what I have learned about the Word of God; how His Word is true and how He does what He promised.

God will give you Supernatural Wisdom, Supernatural Guidance, Supernatural Protection, Supernatural Healing and Supernatural Financial Provision; if you are faithful and obey Gods Word, He will give you all your hearts desires. He knows everything about you; he even knows how many hairs are on your head. He knows what's going to happen before it even happens, so he knows your future and he knows what you need.

Matthew 10: verse 30; "God even knows how many hairs are on you head."

God does indeed work in mysterious ways, with many signs and wonders to follow those who believe. The more you meditate on His Word and spend time with God, the more He will give of Himself to you. I am telling you, it will carry you to a whole new level. The power of God's Word is voice activated; you must speak His Word over your life and others you pray for if you want a miracle or any blessing to manifest!

The anointing of the Holy Spirit is the gateway to Gods Supernatural Power. The miracles I have told you about between my brother and I and the Gift of Prophecy; are a glorious demonstration of the power of God and the Holy Spirit! Just imagine what the entire world would be like and see if everyone were to yield to the precious Holy Spirit!

Understand, the anointing of the Holy Spirit comes through God, He is God, and the Holy Spirit will never force you, He inspires you and He is ever so gentle. He is the Spirit of the Living God, and the Spirit of Truth and He will comfort you and guide you and give peace and wisdom and understanding supernaturally, about the present things in your life and about the future things to come in your life. He is with you always and He is your very best friend, He is your protection because He is a Holy Spirit. Nothing in this world can give you what He can!

The Word of God says: **"In the End Times, The Spirit of the living God (The Holy Spirit) will be known in all the world, like the oceans on the earth."**

When you are facing the impossible or when you are making decisions about your job or your relationships, you don't have to do it on your own. God is interested in every detail of your life, and He has provided direction and guidance in His Word. When life seems dark, or when you aren't sure about which choice to make, turn on the light of God's Word and confess His promises over your life, it chisels away the walls of doubt, fear and uncertainty that would try to block you or hold you back. You will overcome and have victory when you speak God's Word over your situation. God will never fail you! Keep fighting the good fight! If someone you know is sick, or is having a problem of any kind, you should always offer to pray for them.

The Devil looks for people all throughout the earth who don't know the Word of God, so he can devour them! He comes to kill, steal and destroy!

John 10: verse 10; "A thief comes to steal and kill and destroy, but I came to give life–life in all its fullness."

Malachi 3: verse 18; "You will again see the difference between good and evil people, between those who serve God and those who don't."

Colossians 2: verses 13-15; "When you were spiritually dead because of your sins and because you were not free from the power of your sinful self, God made you alive with Christ, and He forgave all your sins. He cancelled the debt, which listed all the rules we failed to follow. He took away that record with its rules and nailed it to the cross. God stripped away spiritual rulers and powers of their authority. With the cross, He won the victory and showed the world that they were powerless."

God's Word is "need specific". If there is any need that you have, God will bless you with it. But you must be faithful. Get familiar with the Bible so you can speak

God's Word over your life. If you don't have a Bible, get one. I recommend the New Testament Amplified Version, or "The Devotional Bible" by Max Lucado; it has a (Where To Go To When' Index) on need specific topics that we encounter in our daily lives that will help you find scripture you need quickly and it's easier to read and understand. Look up the scriptures that apply to the things you need in your life and begin to meditate on those words aloud. And start talking to God and to Jesus and develop your own personal intimate relationship with them, and acknowledge the Holy Spirit if you want His help. If you believe and you are faithful you will be blessed! **"Jesus is the provider, and He is the healer, and He is the Prince of Peace, He is Lord of heaven and earth and God is in control!** When you have Jesus in your life, you can't help but to tell others about Him; let Him show you how good He truly is. God will make a way for you, when there is no way in the natural!

Jeremiah 29: verses 11-14; "I say this because I know what I am planning for you," Says the Lord. I have good plans for you, not plans to hurt you. I will give you hope and a good future. Then you will call my name. You will come to me and pray to me, and I will listen to you. You will search for me. And when you search for me with all your heart, you will find me! I will let you find me, says the Lord."

Acts 13: verse 41; "Listen, you people who doubt! You can wonder and then die. **I will do something in your lifetime that you won't believe even when you are told about it!"**

Doubters spend their time discussing the size of their problems. We lose our joy when we doubt. Joy comes when we believe. Believers seek the blessings that God has promised. What God has said, He will bring to pass because **His Word is true.** God loves you and He is no respecter of persons. What He gives to one person is available for any other.

You are not locked into present circumstances. Seasons change. You change, and circumstances change. If there is anything in your life that is stopping you from getting closer to God; IT NEEDS TO GO! Continue to pursue prosperity, good health and happiness. God wishes that you will have it all and He will help you to get it.

Genesis 12: verses 1-3 & Genesis 13: 1-2; Now the Lord had said to Abram: "Get out of your country, from your family and from your father's house, to a land that I will show you. I will make you a great nation; I will bless you and make your name great; and you shall be a blessing. I will bless those who bless you, and I will curse him who curses you; and in you all the families of the earth shall be blessed."

In order for God to bless Abram, He had to take him out of where he was, and he also had to take where he was out of him! God had a great plan for Abram and his descendants and in order for him to fill this plan, God had to take Abram from his current surroundings. Sometimes we are limited by our circumstances and by the people around us. We are stuck in the same old rut and we need to be shaken up and our eyes opened to all the possibilities that are available to us in the Lord. If we want to walk in the blessings of God, we may have to make some defining choices. We will need to leave the influence and company of those who are negative and destructive and who are leading us away from the plans and purposes God has for us, and press into God for His will to be done in our lives.

Each act of obedience to God's instruction is linked to a blessing or miracle in your life. It is important to make the right move, in the right way, at the right time, for this is how the guidance of the Holy Spirit gives you the edge in every situation with which you are confronted. It is only reasonable to be concerned about the issues we have in our lives, but you can gain strength in knowing you are not alone. I promise you, if you are being led by the Holy Spirit, your lives will be transformed.

Romans 8: verse 5; "Those who live following there sinful selves think only about things their sinful selves want. But those who live following the Spirit are thinking about the things the Spirit wants them to do."

Romans 8: verses 8-9; "Those people who are ruled by their sinful selves cannot please God. But you are not ruled by your sinful selves. You are ruled by the Spirit, if that Spirit of God really lives in you. But the person who does not have the Spirit of Christ does not belong to Christ.

Romans 8: verse 14; "The true children of God are those who let God's Spirit lead them."

1 **Peter 1: verses 5-9;** "God's power protects you through your faith until salvation is shown to you at the end of time. This makes you very happy, even though now for a short time different kinds of troubles may make you sad. These troubles come to prove that your faith is pure. This purity of faith is worth more than gold, which can prove to be pure by fire but will ruin. But the purity of your faith will bring you praise and glory and honor when Jesus Christ is shown to you. You have not seen Christ, but still you love him. You cannot see him now, but you believe in him. So you are filled with joy that cannot be explained, a joy full of glory. And you are receiving the goal of your faith...the salvation of your souls."

1 **Peter 5: verses 6-11;** "Be humble under God's powerful hand so he will lift you up when the right time comes. Give all your worries to him, because he cares about you. Control yourselves and be careful! The devil, your enemy, goes around like a roaring lion looking for someone to eat. Refuse to give in to him, by standing strong in your faith. You know that your Christian family all over the world is having the same kinds of suffering. And after you suffer for a short time, God, who gives all grace, will make everything right. He will make you strong and support you and keep you from falling. He called you to share in his glory in Christ, a glory that will continue forever. All power is His forever and ever. Amen

Kindly humble yourself and acknowledge that **God knows more than you do, and give Him first place in your life;** always speak to God for guidance and wisdom before you make a decision with anything in your life no matter what your need is, because He will guide you. When you stay in the will of God, His plans for you will inevitably come to pass because God does not make mistakes.

God's Word spoken out of your mouth regularly produces a powerful victorious life! I wish someone would have told me this when I was younger.

God always keeps His promise. Lean on Him and trust in Him with your life and be confident in the Lord Jesus and rely upon Him in every way.

There has been a new generation being brought up all over the nation, with people that are radical and on fire for God! **Ephesians 1: verse 10;** "Whose eyes see the world being run from God's perspective and vision, according to His plan to bring heaven and earth together with Christ as the head."

The Power of God is not meant to be confined to the pulpit of the church! All over the world people are being saved and miraculous miracles are happening outside on the streets! Everything I have shared with you about the excessive blessings and miracles I have received from God, either happened to me in my home or outside of the church!

Romans 2: verse 11; "For God judges all people in the same way."

God is no respecter of persons; the Supernatural Power of God is available to anyone and everyone who wants it! Recently, I have seen children from the ages of five years old and up, being touched by God and filled with the anointing of the Holy Spirit with the evidence of speaking in tongues, (other languages). It does not matter what your age is, we are all God's children and he loves us so very much and wants us to be blessed!

If you will just keep abiding in Him and seek Him with ALL your heart, pray to Him and call upon Him. Then He promises us that He will hear us and answer us. Just keep meditating on His Word. He'll bring you through. He'll make you strong. He'll keep you stable, and you'll embrace the life of excessive blessings He has prepared for you! No matter what we go through, we know that God will have the final say, and His good plans for us WILL succeed! Nothing in this world can give you what He can!

Jeremiah 23: verses 23-24; "I am a God who is near," says the Lord, "I am also a God who is far away." No one can hide where I cannot see him," says the Lord. "I fill all of heaven and earth," says the Lord."

17

~

JESUS IS COMING SOON

God is moving by His Spirit in this land like never before, because **we are living in the last of the last days...The End Times!** You will see the Supernatural Power of God displayed and the Power of the Holy Spirit with your own eyes! Some of the greatest moves of God's miracles, signs and wonders will and are being seen in and outside of the four walls of a church and on the streets today, it has already begun!

Before Jesus left the earth and went up to heaven, he did not leave us to fend for ourselves. He promised to send us the Holy Spirit, the Spirit of the Living God, to live within us, to comfort us, to give us wisdom and guidance with great peace and joy! Jesus wants you to go to Him. He wants to become the most important person in your life, the greatest love you'll ever know. He wants you to love him so much that there's no room in your heart and in your life for sin. Invite Him to live in your heart today.

Revelation 3: verses 15-16 & 19; "I know what you do, that you are not hot or cold. I wish that you were hot or cold! But because you are lukewarm...neither hot nor cold...I am ready to spit you out of my mouth." "I correct and punish those whom I love. So be eager to do right, and change your hearts and lives."

God can't stomach lukewarm faith. He is angered by a religion that puts on a show but ignores the service.

1 Thessalonians 4: verses 16-18; "The Lord himself will come down from heaven with a loud command, with the voice of the archangel, and with the trumpet call of God. And those who have died believing in Christ will rise first. After that, we who are still alive will be gathered up with them in the clouds to meet the Lord in the air. And we will be with the Lord forever. So encourage each other with these words."

1 Thessalonians 5: verses 2-11; "You know very well that the day the Lord comes again will be a surprise, like a thief that comes in the night. While people are saying, "We have peace and we are safe," they will be destroyed quickly. It is like pains that come quickly to a woman having a baby. Those people will not escape. But you, brother and sisters, are not living in darkness, and so that day will not surprise you like a thief. You are all people who belong to the light and to the day. We do not belong to the night or to darkness. So we should not be like other people who are sleeping, but we should be alert and have self-control. Those who sleep, sleep at night. Those who get drunk, get drunk at night. But we belong to the day, so we should control ourselves. We should wear faith and love to protect us, and the hope of salvation should be our helmet.

These are not normal times; the broader economic situation the world faces today is growing more ominous by the moment.

As a Christian with a Bible in his hand surveys the world scene, he is aware that we do not worship an absentee God. He is aware that God is in the shadows of history and that He has a plan. God is always working behind the scenes, even if you can't see it yet. We are getting ready for a Supernatural Deliverance like the world has never seen before! God is in charge of every nation and every army! He will demonstrate His Power one last time!!!

The Christian is not to be disturbed by the chaos, violence, strife, bloodshed, and threat of terrorist and war that fill the pages of our daily newspapers. We know that these things are the consequences of sin and greed. Every day we see a thousand evidences of the fulfillment of the Biblical Prophecy. Every day as I read the Newspaper I say; "The Bible is true." No matter how foreboding the future, the Christian knows the end of the story. We are heading towards a glorious climax. "The best is yet to come!" The Bible indicates that the future is in God's hands. The future is in the hands of One who is preparing something greater than the eye hath seen or the ear heard, or had entered into the heart of man to conceive. (By Max Lucado) **Yes, God is in control.**

Heaven is where the believers go when they leave this earth!

John wrote Revelations to tell us about what he was shown by an angel, and to encourage Christians to stand firm during persecution. Jesus, the Mighty One, cares for us and stands with us. No matter what we face, He gives us His love and power.

John Sees Heaven

Revelation 4: verses 2-11; "Immediately I was in the Spirit, and before me was a throne in heaven, and someone was sitting on it. The One who sat on the throne looked like precious stones, like jasper and carnelian. All around the throne was a rainbow the color of an emerald. Around the throne there were twenty-four other thrones with twenty-four elders sitting on them. They were dressed in white and had golden crowns on their head.

Lightning flashes and noises and thundering came from the throne. Before the throne seven lamps were burning, which are the seven Spirits of God. Also before the throne there was something that looked like a sea of glass, clear like crystal.

In the center and around the throne were four living creatures with eyes all over them, in front and in back. The first living creature was like a lion. The second was like a calf. The third had a face like a man. The fourth was like a flying eagle. Each of these four living creatures had six wings and was covered all over with eyes, inside and out. Day and night they never stop saying; "Holy, Holy, Holy is the Lord God Almighty. He was, he is, and he is coming."

These living creatures give glory, honor, and thanks to the One who sits on the throne, who lives forever and ever. Then the twenty-four elders bow down before the One who sits on the throne, and they worship him who lives forever and ever. They put their crowns down before the throne and say; "You are worthy, our Lord and God, to receive glory and honor and power, because you made all things. Everything existed and was made, because you wanted it.

Revelation 21: verses 1-27; "Then I saw a new heaven and a new earth, for the first heaven and the first earth had passed away, and the sea was no more. And I saw the holy city, New Jerusalem, coming down out of heaven from God, prepared as a bride adorned for her husband. And I heard a loud voice from the throne saying, "Now God's presence is with people, and he will live with them, and they will be his people. God himself will be with them and he will be their God. He will wipe away every tear from their eyes, and there will be no more death, sadness, crying, or pain because all the old ways are gone."

"The one sitting on the throne said, "Look! I am making everything new!" Then he said, "Write this, because these words are true and can be trusted."

The one on the throne said to me, "It is finished. I am the **Alpha** and the **Omega," the Beginning and the End**. I will give free water from the spring of life to anyone who is thirsty. Those who win victory will receive this, and I will be their God and they will be my children. But cowards, those who refuse to believe, who do evil things, who kill, who sin sexually, who do evil magic, who worship idols, and who tell lies – all these will have a place in the lake of burning sulfur. This is the second death."

"Then one of seven angels who had the seven bowls full of seven last troubles come to me saying, "Come with me and I will show you the Bride, the wife of the Lamb." And the angel carried me away by the Spirit to a very large and high mountain. He showed me the Holy city, Jerusalem coming down out of heaven from God. It was shining with the glory of God and was bright like a very expensive jewel, like jasper, clear as crystal. The city a great high wall and with twelve gates with twelve angels at the gates, and on each gate was written the names of the twelve tribes of Israel. There were three gates on north, three gates on the south, three gates on the east and three gates on the west. The walls of the city were built on twelve foundation stones, and on the stones were written the names of the twelve apostles of the Lamb. The angel who talked with me had a measuring rod made of gold to measure the city, its gates, and its wall. The city was built in a square, and its length was equal to its width. The angel measured the city with the rod. The city was twelve thousand stadia" long, twelve thousand stadia wide, and twelve thousand stadia high.

The angel also measured the wall. It was one hundred forty-four cubits" high, by human measurements, which the angel was using.

The wall was made of jasper, and the city was made of pure gold, as pure as glass. The foundation stones of the city walls were decorated with every kind of jewel. The first foundation was jasper, the second was sapphire, the third was chalcedony, the fourth was emerald, the fifth was onyx, the sixth was carnelian, the seventh was chrysolite, the eighth was beryl, the ninth was topaz, the tenth was crysoprase, the eleventh was jacinth, and the twelfth was amethyst. The twelve gates were twelve pearls, each gate having been made from a single pearl. And the street of the city was made of pure gold as clear as glass.

I did not see a temple in the city, because the Lord God Almighty and the Lamb are the city's temple. The city does not need the sun or the moon to shine on it, because the glory of God is its light, and the Lamb is the city's lamp. By its light the people of the world will walk, and the king of the earth will bring their glory into it. The city gates will never be shut on any day, because there is no night there. The glory and the honor of the nations will be brought into it. Nothing unclean and no one who does shameful things or tells lies will ever go into it. Only those whose names are written in the Lamb's book of life will enter the city."

What a vision that must have been. It gives us some idea of what heaven is like, and now we can only imagine how wonderful it must be.

Why do Jesus and his angels rejoice over one repenting sinner? Can they see something we can't? Do they know something we don't? Absolutely. They know what heaven holds. They've seen the table, and they've heard the music, and they can't wait to see your face when you arrive. Better still, they can't wait to see you. When you arrive and enter the party, something wonderful will happen. A final transformation will occur. You will be just like Jesus. Drink deeply from **1 John 3: verse** 2; "We have not yet been shown what we will be in the future. But we know that when Christ comes again, *we will be like him.*" Of all the blessings of heaven one of the greatest will be you! You will be God's magnum opus, his work of art. The angels will gasp. God's work will be completed. At last, you will have a heart like his. You will love with a perfect love. You will worship with a radiant face. You'll hear each word God speaks. Your heart will be pure, your words will be like jewels, and your thoughts will be like treasures.

You will be just like Jesus. You will, at long last, have a heart just like his. Envision the heart of Jesus and you'll be envisioning your own. Guiltless. Fearless. Thrilled and joyous. Tirelessly worshiping. Flawlessly discerning. As the mountain stream is pristine and endless, so will be your heart. You will be like Him.

And if that were not enough, everyone else will be like him as well. "Heaven is the perfect place for people made perfect." Heaven is populated by those who let God change them. Arguments will cease, for jealousy won't exist. Suspicions won't surface, for there will be no secrets. Every sin is gone. Every insecurity is forgotten. Every fear is past. Pure wheat. No weeds. Pure gold. No alloy. Pure love. No lust. Pure hope. No fear. No wonder the angels rejoice when one sinner repents; they know another work of art will soon grace the gallery of God. They know what heaven holds. (From *Just like Jesus* by Max Lucado)

Before Jesus returned to heaven, he promised that he was going to prepare a place for us...in one of His Father's Mansions! He is waiting for the perfect time for us all to be together.

Matthew 24: verses 36-44; "No one knows when the day or the time will be, not the angels in heaven, not even the Son. Only the Father knows. When the Son of Man comes, it will be like what happened in Noah's time. In those days before the flood, people were eating and drinking, marrying and giving their children to be married, until the day Noah entered the boat. They knew nothing about what was happening until the flood came and destroyed them. It will be the same when the Son of Man comes. Two men will be in the field. One will be taken, and the other will be left. Two women will be grinding grain with a mill. One will be taken, and the other will be left. **So always be ready, because you don't know the day the Lord will come.** Remember this: If the owner of the house knew what time of the night the thief was coming, the owner would watch and not let the thief break in. **So you also must be ready, because the Son of Man will come at a time you don't expect him."**

If you have ever been skeptical about whether God is real and Jesus is alive and living in heaven; don't be anymore! It is my prayer that this True Story I share with you; will touch every person's life and cause you to repent of your sins and your souls to be saved by accepting Jesus Christ as your Lord and Savior. He is LORD of heaven and earth. He is the greatest LOVE you will ever know; He is the lover of your soul. And He is coming soon!

I have only shared a few of the things I have prophesied through the Holy Spirit, because they are mostly about my personal life. However, I did prophesy these words on April 26, 2012, and I feel a since of urgency to share this Prophetic Word with you. I spoke these words over and over again:

"People of God will live to see the Lord come again." "Get ready!"

(I believe this means that Jesus will come again in our lifetime!)

I'm ready, are you? "The Final Countdown Has Begun!

John reported that Jesus Christ would initiate the final conflict against Satan. At the end, God would defeat Satan and throw him into hell.

Revelation 22: verse 6; "These words can be trusted and are true." The Lord, the God of the Spirits of the prophets, sent his angel to show his servants the things that must happen soon."

Revelation 22: verses 12-13; "Listen! I am coming soon! I will bring my reward with me, and I will repay each one of you for what you have done. I am the Alpha and the Omega, the First and the Last, the Beginning and the End. "I am the Almighty."

God often uses some of our deepest pain, as the launching pad of our greatest calling. Even in the midst of your hurting you can be comforted in your pain, knowing that God will take even that pain and do something wonderful and beautiful in you through that.

It is a great privilege and honor to share my testimonies with you, because faith comes by hearing and seeing. Please learn to trust in God, our Lord Jesus Christ and the precious life changing fellowship of the Holy Spirit. We are living in unusual times. **Those that survive and come out on top will be those who are led by the Holy Spirit. It is through the Gifts of the Spirit that we are able to know things that the devil does not know.** Allow the anointing of the Holy Spirit to come into your life by asking God for it; you will never be the same again. You will be transformed; great miracles will happen and become a daily common occurrence in your life!

Psalm 91: verses 9-11 and 14- 16; "**The Lord is your protection**; you have made God Most High your place of safety. Nothing bad will happen to you; no disaster will come to your home. He has put his angels in charge of you to watch over you wherever you go." The Lord says, "Whoever loves me, I will save. I will protect those who know me. They will call to me, and I will answer them. I will be with them in trouble; I will rescue them and honor them. I will give them a long, full life, and they will see how I can save."

Psalm 117: verses 1-2; "All you nations praise the Lord. All you people, praise Him because the Lord loves us very much, and his truth is everlasting."

James 5: verses 7-11; "Brothers and sisters be patient until the Lord comes again. Do not give up hope, because the Lord is coming soon."

The Words of Scripture are alive; they are saturated with the power of God. So speak the Word of God over your life and activate His power in every situation! The truth is you can't do it without Him!

Mark 16: verse 15; "Go into all the world and teach the gospel to all creations."

Gods anointing on you is more important than your talent, your education or what family you come from.

If you take the limits off of God; He will amaze you with His goodness. He'll not only meet your needs, he'll give you the desires of your heart. He wants us to live an exciting and fulfilling and joyful life! Don't be satisfied with a mediocre, okay, barely-get-along life. If you settle for that, that's all you're going to get! Go for the very best life God has for you. He is a God of excessive blessings!

When God blesses you, it will always come in a way different from anything you could ever dream or imagined. Look what happened to me; it is God who laid it upon my heart and gave me the desire to write this book about what He has done in my life, to honor Him and give Him the glory, and to enhance your relationship with Him. If you are not following Jesus, it's because you don't know how or you are not willing. And that's exactly why I am so passionate about sharing my story with you, to challenge you to stand on God's Word and see what He will do for you; it will always be far greater than anything you could have ever done or imagined on your own!

Every miracle and blessing that I share with you in this book, are specific prayers I asked of God that He honored! When you look back at the chronological order of how God lined everything up; all the blessings and miracles, signs and wonders God gave me...you will understand how great and wonderful His love truly is, and how everything He does is very personal and always in perfect timing.

I'll say it again; God meets you at the level of your expectation. When you have "Now Faith" and go through your day with expectancy, you'll see God show up in amazing ways!

Hebrews 11: verse 1; "Now faith is the assurance of things hoped for and knowing that something is real even if we do not see it."

God is turning up the volume with His power to show everyone He is real and alive! God's highest passion is to get his children home. This is only the beginning of the great miracles, signs and wonders this nation will see in these last days of which we are living; what steps can you take this next year to influence others for the kingdom? It is those Christians who are thinking of our next life (eternal life in heaven) that are the most effective in this one.

Hebrews 10: verses 32 & 35-39; "Remember those days in the past when you first learned the truth. You had a hard struggle with many sufferings, but you continued strong." "So do not lose the courage you had in the past, which has a great reward. You must hold on so you can do what God wants and receive what he has promised. For in a very short time, "The One who is coming will come and will not be delayed. The person who is right with me will live by trusting in me. But if he turns back with fear, I will not be pleased with him." But we are not those who turn back and are lost. We are people who have faith and are saved.

2 Timothy 4: verses 7-8; "I have fought the good fight, I have finished the race, I have kept my faith. Now, a crown is being held for me...a crown for being right with God. The Lord, the judge who judges rightly, will give the crown to me on that day," "not only to me but to all those who have waited with love for him to come again."

Don't let anyone steal your crown, the Crown of Righteousness', the overcomers crown for being right with God and living a pure life.

1 Thessalonians 5: verses 12-13 & 16-23; "Now, brothers and sisters, we ask you to appreciate those who work hard among you, who lead you in the Lord and teach you. Respect them with a very special love because of the work they do. Always be joyful. Pray continually, and give thanks whatever happens. That is what God wants for you in Christ Jesus." "Do not hold back the work of the Holy Spirit. Do not treat prophecy as if it were unimportant. But test everything. Keep what is good, and stay away from evil. Now may God himself, the God of peace, make you pure, belonging only to Him. May your whole self...spirit, soul, and body be kept safe and without fault when our Lord Jesus Christ comes."

Daniel 12: verse 3; "The wise people will shine like the brightness of the sky. Those who teach others to live right will shine like stars forever and ever."

Malachi 4: verses 1-3; "There is a day coming that will burn like a hot furnace, and all the proud and evil people will be like straw. On that day they will be completely burned up so that not a root or branch will be left," says the Lord All-Powerful. But for you who honor me, goodness will shine on you like the sun, with healing in its rays. You will jump around like well-fed calves.

Then you will crush the wicked like ashes under your feet on the day I will do this," says the Lord All-Powerful.""

Matthew 28: verses 18-29; "Then Jesus came to them and said, "All power in heaven and on earth is given to me. So go and make followers of all people in the world. Baptize them in the name of the Father and of the Son and the Holy Spirit. Teach them to obey everything that I have taught you, and I will be with you always, even until the end of age."

Jesus followers are not to be bound by religion and tradition...but to be an influence to turn people's lives around. A "Disciple" is someone who is productive in connecting others with God. It is seriously time to go to the next level and see the miraculous power that God has given us the authority to use for miracles and to do something specific for the kingdom.

You haven't seen excitement, until you hook-up with the plan of God on your life! God is making people multi-millionaires to fund the End Time Harvest! God will do things through you that will astound your family and friends! God has a plan to shake America, and He wants to use each and every one of you to save millions of lost people before Jesus comes again!

Jesus Coming' is mentioned three hundred times in the New Testament. Nothing will matter more, than the people you take to heaven with you! The Bible says that those who know their God will do exploits in His name! These are the days of the people who are Spirit filled and radical believers with the understanding of God and what He can do, and especially in these last of the last days... it is very exciting to know we can be used of God according to the power at work within us by His Spirit to save a lost and dying world!

Keep your since of urgency and stay Spirit filled, and please kindly inform everyone you know about this phenomenal True Story of God's profound and unique miracles from heaven, so they may be blessed too. Your doing so...will cause many souls to be saved for the kingdom of heaven and many kinds of miracles to take place for those who need them.

Matthew 4: verse 19; "Follow me Jesus said; and I will make you fishers of men!"

When you get down to the heart of the matter, it's all about souls. And the only way we're going to populate heaven is to "Save Souls", we must move quickly! Jesus is coming very soon!

John 15: verses 7-9; "IF YOU REMAIN IN ME, AND MY WORDS REMAIN IN YOU. ASK WHATEVER YOU WISH and it will be done FOR YOU." You should produce much fruit and show you are my followers, which brings glory to my Father. I loved you as the Father loved me... NOW REMAIN IN MY LOVE."

Thank you wonderful Lord Jesus!

May God bless you excessively, and give you all your hearts desires...

In Jesus wonderful Holy name, Amen.

BROTHER

Our hearts ache in sadness and secret tears still flow.

What it meant to lose you no one will ever know.

When we are sad and lonely and everything goes wrong;

We seem to hear you whisper "Cheer up and carry on."

Each time we see your picture, you seem to smile and say,

"Don't cry I'm up in heaven we'll meet again someday."